Yale Strom

UNCERTAIN ROADS

Searching for the Gypsies

Four Winds Press ❈ *New York*

Maxwell Macmillan Canada   *Toronto*   Maxwell Macmillan International   *New York   Oxford   Singapore   Sydney*

10 9 8 7 6 5 4 3 2 1
The text of this book is set in ITC Galliard.
Maps by Virginia Norey   Calligraphy by Edward R. Heins
Book design by Christy Hale
Library of Congress Cataloging-in-Publication Data   Strom, Yale. Uncertain roads : searching for the gypsies / Yale Strom.—1st ed.   p.   cm. Includes bibliographical references (p.). Summary: Includes interviews with several generations of gypsies living in Sweden, Hungary, Romania, and the Ukraine today. ISBN 0-02-788531-3 1. Gypsies—Europe—Interviews—Juvenile literature. 2. Europe—Ethnic relations—Juvenile literature. [1. Gypsies—Europe—Interviews.] I. Title. DX115.S87   1993   305.8'0094—dc20 92-21962

ACKNOWLEDGMENTS

I would like to thank the following people, who helped to make this book possible. First I thank Anna Safran of Täby; Rysiek Solarz, Toni Kwik Atanasio, Steve Atanasio, Sonya Atanasio, and George Iliuta of Stockholm; Karl-Gunnar and Margareta Olsson of Lund; Pukla Lakatos of Malmö; Laszlo and Edit Fekete, Ferenc Javori, Bob Cohen, Andras Racz, Daniel Erdély, and Tivados Foityol of Budapest; Andras Klein György of Nyíregyháza; János and Julia Kobrin, Judita and Anton Gergelyi of Vinogradov; Carmen and Adrian Şipoş and Ioana Osoiana of Cluj-Napoca. All of these people provided me with invaluable help and hospitality. I also thank the following for their assistance in translating the interviews and music text: Vera Eisenberger, Julian Şerer, and Joasia Swiecicki-Strom. I thank, too, John Nickels for his translation of the Romani lyrics, and Ismail Butera and Karen Elaine for their musical arrangements. Special thanks to J's lab in Oak Park, Michigan, for its careful work in printing the photographs. I thank those who had researched the Rom prior to my travels and were able to give me scholarly advice: Gabriella Trynauer, Toby Sonneman, Marlene Sway, and Dr. Ian Hancock. I express extreme gratitude to my agent, Mary Jack Wald; friend and art director, Christy Hale; and my parents, David and Phyllis. Most of all, I thank my editor and friend, Virginia Duncan, whose insight, encouragement, and enthusiasm for the project pushed me to a clear and focused end.

TABLE OF CONTENTS

*To the hundreds of thousands of forgotten Rom
who tragically lost their lives in the Holocaust*

A NOTE FROM THE AUTHOR

Today there are approximately ten million to eleven million Rom living in Europe—including the Baltic countries, Russia, Ukraine, and Turkey. With the collapse of communism, the fall of the Berlin Wall, and the reunification of Germany, Pandora's box has been opened, and its contents—nationalism, pan-Slavism, tribalism, and anti-Semitism—have created an atmosphere of intolerance.

The most easily identifiable targets for this backlash are the Rom. Recently Rom families have been burned out of their homes in several Romanian villages. In the former Eastern Bloc countries, Rom have been excluded from claiming farmland as the plots of state agricultural cooperatives have been distributed among farmers. Bias attacks against the Rom have risen in Germany, Poland, the Czech Republic, Slovakia, Hungary, and Romania.

Even in music, hatred of the Rom is finding explicit expression. Fans of the rightist and neo-Nazi music known as Oi (derived from punk, with some heavy-metal influences) can be found throughout Europe. In Hungary the skinhead band CPG, which stands for *Cigany Puszitito Garda*, or Gypsy Exterminators Regiment, plays to crowded houses. In the song "Gypsy Free Zone," the band sings:

> *The flame-thrower is the weapon*
> *with which I can triumph,*
> *Exterminate the Gypsies*
> *Whether child, woman, or man.*

Here in the United States we perpetuate ignorance and intolerance of the estimated one million Rom living among us. Just think, for example, of the ways in which we use the word *Gypsy* in our everyday language. For example, the term *Gypsy cabdriver* is not used to describe a driver's ethnicity but rather to label someone who picks up passengers without a proper taxi license. The parasitic Gypsy moth, whose larvae feed on the foliage of trees, was not given that name accidentally. And the word *gyp*, meaning to swindle or cheat, is used commonly in our conversations.

Most of us at some point have fantasized about traveling with the Gypsies; joining a caravan—if only for a short time—to venture down uncertain and mysterious roads. I will always cherish the time I spent with the Rom you will meet in this book—remembering especially their humor, hospitality, and haunting melodies. The words and pictures on the following pages reveal the fears, hopes, ideas, and customs of a beautiful people whose culture has enriched the world.

To travel is to dream.
YALE STROM
New York, 1993

Rinkeby, Sweden: Rom teenagers hanging out

INTRODUCTION

For many people the word *Gypsy* evokes an air of mystery and romance as well as scenes of dancing, fortune-telling, music and brightly colored caravans of carriages pulled by horses. Many people also think of filth, dishonesty, and crime.

In this book the Gypsies will be referred to as the Rom. This is their proper name, the name they use to refer to themselves. The Rom share a common language called Romani. In Romani the name for all people who are not Rom is *gaje*.

Who are the Rom? Where do they come from? How did they come to live in all of the countries in Europe and in many other countries around the world? What is the mystery surrounding them that makes the *gaje* so wary and suspicious of them?

There are many legends concerning the origins of the Rom. Many of these legends, told by the Rom themselves, were intended to ingratiate the Rom with the Europeans. The following is a legend that has been told as *parameetchi* (Rom sagas told orally) for generations.

It is said that three different Jewish blacksmiths refused a request by some Roman soldiers in Jerusalem to forge the four spikes that were to be used in crucifying Jesus, the son of Mary. The Romans killed the Jewish blacksmiths. Outside the gates of Jerusalem the soldiers met a Rom who had just pitched his tent and set up his anvil, and they hired him to do the job. After the third spike was forged there came a rumbling sound from the sky. When the rumbling stopped the Rom and the Roman soldiers heard the trembling voices of the three Jewish blacksmiths pleading with the Rom not to make the fourth spike. The soldiers were frightened and ran away before the last spike was made. When the Rom had finished the spike he went to cool it in a bucket of water but the iron remained hot and red. The blacksmith tried desperately to cool off the spike, but it continued to glow fiery red. Terrified and trembling, the Rom dropped the spike, packed his tent upon his donkey, and fled into the desert. At nightfall the Rom decided to rest his donkey. When he sat down on the ground he saw the glowing spike sizzling in the sand. Crazed with fear, the Rom traveled farther into the desert. From then on whenever he lit his forge the burning spike appeared. And it appeared to all his descendants. This is why the Rom move from one place to another and why Jesus was crucified with only three spikes. His two feet were drawn together and one spike pierced them. The fourth spike still wanders the earth.

All of what we know today about the history of the Rom comes from studying their language. Their language and memories were the only "books" the Rom took when they left India. The idea that the Rom are generally illiterate stems from the fact that they did not record their history.

Of the many tribes that still exist in India today, the Rom probably descend from the Luri and Dom tribes. The Dom (where the word *Rom* most likely comes from) earned their living as musicians, entertainers, and metalsmiths. They were the only tribe to work with iron in ancient India because, according to the Hindu religion, iron was considered dangerous and impure to handle. The Dom were a very low caste, and they were nomadic. With dark skin and Aryan features they wandered from the south to the north of India, singing and playing the drums. In Sanskrit the word *Dom* means "to resound." The Dom were some of the earliest pariahs in In-

dia. The word *pariah*, meaning one deprived of all religious or social rights, a member of the lowest or no caste, or an outcast from society, comes from the Tamil word *parai* (drum), and a *paraiyar* was a drummer. After one hundred years of forced servitude this group of Rom dispersed, some traveling northward and others southwestward.

The disintegration of the Indian empire in the seventh century brought wave upon wave of conquering armies, which swept through India and eventually into Europe. In the midst of invasions during the seventh to twelfth centuries by the Greeks, Persians, Muslims, and Genghis Khan, many Rom were forced to leave India. They created a diaspora like that of the Jews, beginning an exodus that continues to this day.

Leaving the banks of the Indus River, the Rom split into two groups. One group followed the Indus north, crossing the Sulaiman Mountains, first into Afghanistan, then into Persia, and eventually across Anatolia into Turkey. The second group traveled southwest and followed the coastline of the Arabian Sea toward the Persian Gulf. Some of these Rom split off into a third group. Part of the tribe continued north through Azerbaijan, Armenia, and eventually into Russia. The other part of the group continued through Persia, Iraq, into Syria, and then followed the southern Mediterranean coastline all along North Africa into Spain.

Because the Rom left no written records of their wanderings, linguists have used non-Romani names and words that were adopted by them to trace their travels. For example, the presence of many Armenian, Persian, and Greek words in Romani proves that the Rom stayed in the Byzantine Empire for a considerable time. Also, officials in some European towns and regions did record information about where the Rom had traveled from and where they were going.

By the time the Ottoman armies had conquered Thrace (1365), Bulgaria (1366), and southern Serbia (1389), the Rom inhabited all of the Balkans. At the beginning of the fifteenth century the Rom were spread throughout Central Europe, and by the end of the sixteenth century they could be found in all of Europe.

The Rom were called different names by the indigenous peoples of each country they traveled through. Some of these names have astonishing origins. For example, the Persians called the Rom *Karaki*, and the French in lower Provence, *Caraque*. The root word for both of these names is *kara* (common to all languages of the Near East), which means "black" in Tatar. The Rom were originally dark-skinned people. The Georgian monks wrote of the *Atsincani*, a term that most probably came from the Greek word *athigganein* ("not to touch"). Gradually, popular pronunciation corrupted the word into *atsingaeim*, which evolved into the most common names in Europe for the Rom: *Tchinghanie* (Turkey), *Tsigani* (Bulgaria), *Tigani* (Romania), *Ciganyok* (Hungary), *Zingari* (Italy), *Zigeuner* (Germany), *Zincali* and *Gitanos* (Spain), *Ciganos* (Portugal), *Zigenare* (Sweden), and *Tzingan* (Russia).

The Rom may have originated in Egypt and that story gives us the terms *Egiftos* (Greece), *Evgit* (Albania), *Gyptanaers* (Holland), *Gypsies* (English), and another name in Hungarian, *Pharaoah-Nepek* (Pharoah's people). The Germans also called them *Tatern*, and the Swedes called them *Tattare*, from the word *Tartar*, thinking these dark-skinned wanderers who spoke an unfamiliar language and wore exotic clothing were part of the Tatar tribe.

The prejudices against the Rom were just as varied as their names. When the Turks were conquering the vast areas between Persia and Asia Minor, many Rom were forced to convert to Islam, while others were chased from their homes. During the Crusades, between the eleventh and thirteenth centuries, Europeans associated the "strange-looking" Rom with the warring Tatars and Turks, who were their enemies. The Europeans then revived the legend about a Rom blacksmith who cast the spikes that were used to crucify Jesus. This legend helped reinforce the view that the Rom were heathens and heretics, people who were the devil's agents and worked in fortune-telling, witchcraft, and black magic. Consequently, in the folklore and history of each European country, one reads that the Rom were often identified with the various nomadic people of the day who earned a living by taking alms: vagabonds, beggars, and itinerant minstrels.

Discrimination became worse for the Rom in the Middle Ages. In the late fourteenth century in Romania and parts of Serbia they became slaves of the landowners, knights, and the Church, and were not emancipated until 1864. Throughout Europe in the fifteenth century the Inquisition murdered thousands of innocent people. The Spanish Inquisition instituted by King Ferdinand and Queen Isabella in 1478 was the most feared of all. Jews, Muslims, and Rom, accused of being infidels, were tried, imprisoned, exiled, or burned at the stake. Soon afterward François I of France, Emperor Maximilian I of Germany, Henry VIII of England, Christian III of Denmark, and Gustav Vasa of Sweden followed the lead of the Spanish court and severely persecuted the Rom.

Wherever the Rom traveled and set up camp, laws established by the *gaje*

soon resulted in their imprisonment or expulsion. Ironically, a few individual Rom—musicians, dancers, singers, fortune-tellers, and metalsmiths—were accepted by some members of the royalty and aristocracy, beginning in the eighteenth century. The Rom and their wanderlust were romanticized in painting, poetry, and literature. But most Rom during this time were forced to live in misery and squalor on the outskirts of towns; thus, many took to stealing as a means to survive. Consequently, any Rom was seen as a thieving Rom, and this idea still persists today.

Finally, the darkest cloud of all, the rise of the Third Reich, engulfed the Rom of Europe. The hangman's noose began to tighten with the Nuremberg Race Laws of 1935, which declared the Rom and Jews to be second-class citizens (having "alien" blood). Considered asocial and parasitic people, the Rom were earmarked for extinction in Hitler's Final Solution. Only the Jews and the Rom—among all of Europe's religious and ethnic groups—were singled out by the Nazis for total annihilation. By the end of World War II, more than half a million Rom had been systematically murdered. Some were shot and others were beaten or died from disease and hunger, while the rest were gassed in several concentration camps, including Auschwitz.

After the war, and for the next thirty

years, the world—and especially the German government—denied the Rom's ordeal during the Holocaust. There were no monuments, no international conferences, and few reparations paid to Rom victims by the German government. Unlike the Jewish experience, the Rom tragedy had become the "forgotten Holocaust." Finally, in 1979, the International Romani Union, made up of seventy-one Rom associations in twenty-seven countries, was granted permanent representation in the United Nations. Then, in 1987, the Reagan administration appointed a Rom to be an official member of the U.S. Holocaust Memorial Council, which, among other things, was involved in constructing the U.S. Memorial Holocaust Museum in Washington. Though the process has been painfully slow, the silent plight of the Rom during World War II and their continued persecution, particularly in Central and Eastern Europe, even after the destruction of the Berlin Wall, has begun to pierce the world's consciousness. As one Rom I interviewed succinctly said, "We are flesh and blood, and God is flesh and blood. Love and reasoning rule God's deeds; nature and the universe rule man's deeds. We are life itself."

Rinkeby, Sweden: Diverse beauty among the Rom

Hodász, Hungary: One of the Rom patriarchs of the community, proudly holding his granddaughter

Map by Virginia Norey

These are the probable routes the Rom took as they migrated westward from their homeland in India.

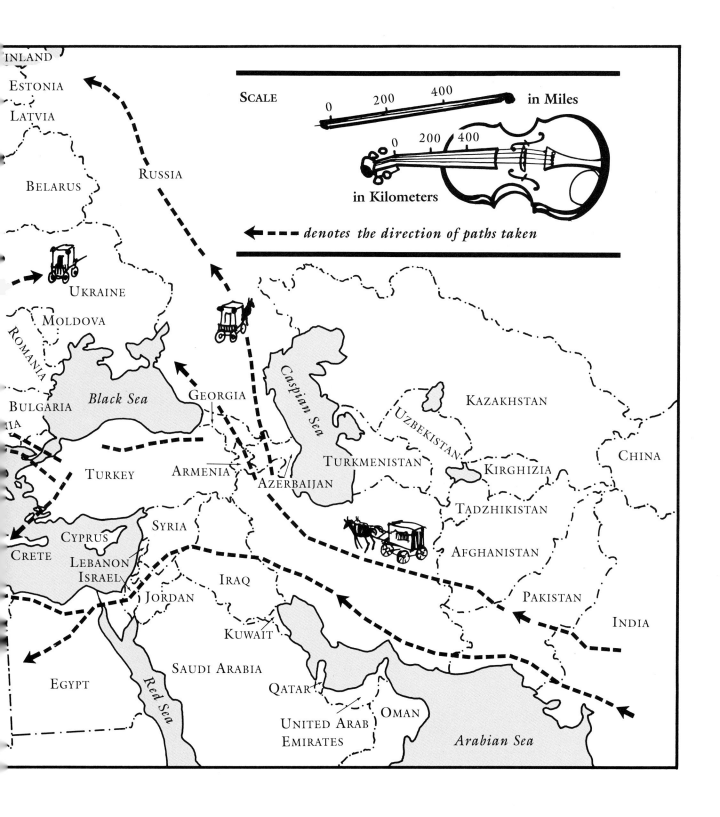

Cluj, Romania: An old Rom circus in the Oşer (a suburb of Cluj) market

ROMANIA

t is thought that the Rom first appeared in Moldavia (today Moldova) and Wallachia (today Romania) in 1417. At the time these two provinces were vassal states of the Ottoman Empire. Both provinces had endured six centuries of successive invasions by the warring armies of the Huns, Arabs, Tatars, Slavs, and finally the Turks. In part of the Ottoman Empire the Turks allowed the Church, princes, and Orthodox clergy to govern the inhabitants, and they in turn affirmed rigorous control over two of their largest minorities: the Rom and the Jews. The majority of the Rom were illiterate and, unlike the Jews, the Rom were forced into slavery.

The Rom slaves were sold by public auction in slave markets, where men and women had to stand naked in complete humiliation as the prospective bidders prodded and probed at them. The Rom lived in inhuman conditions, received no wages, and ate poorly. If they tried to escape or were blamed (justly or unjustly) for doing something they were not supposed to do, they were beaten and often made to stand in a bucket of cold water for twenty-four hours.

Some Rom managed to escape to the Carpathian Mountains, where they lived in the forests and caves, enduring the cold winters with some help from the equally poor peasants and woodcutters. So inhospitable was this uncharted terrain that the Romanian soldiers rarely ventured after the Rom.

Slavery was officially abolished (though in some rural areas it remained) in 1851 because of the French-inspired Romanian Revolution of 1848. The creation of the kingdom of Romania in 1861 helped to end all Rom slavery by 1864. For a brief time there was an official tolerance of the Rom. Many gathered in groups according to the skills they had known or acquired and settled in the outskirts of several big towns. Some of these occupations were metalworking, horse breaking, wood carving, and bear taming. Others began their nomadic ways again and spread throughout the country. The tolerance of the government and of the *gaje* faded quickly. By the 1880s the Rom (as well as the Jews) were being branded as aliens and vagrants and denied the rights of residence and occupation. Consequently, between the years of 1881 and 1924 many thousands of Rom from Ro-

Transylvania, Romania: Horses grazing in the hills

mania, Hungary, Slovakia, and Serbia immigrated to the United States. Today the majority of the Rom in the United States are descended from those Rom émigrés.

The saddest time for the Rom in Romanian history came during World War II, when over 35,000 Rom were murdered by the Nazi and Romanian soldiers. Many of those killed died in the concentration camps established in the Transnistria region of the Ukraine.

During the Communist years assimilation of the Rom was a high priority for the government. Already less than half of the Rom spoke Romani. The Rom language, banned by slave owners, had all but vanished during the centuries of slavery. The Communists hoped that by integrating the Rom into Romanian society their culture, customs, and language would gradually disappear altogether. According to a Rom I interviewed it was just a more "civilized form of the Holocaust."

In the Ceauşcscu years (1965–1989) the Rom learned how to live in both their own world and the *gajo's*. Many obeyed Communist laws and did some of the work the authorities demanded of them (usually hard and menial labor jobs), while others managed to work for themselves buying and selling smuggled goods in the lucrative black market. Other Rom took advantage of Ceauşescu's various political idiosyncrasies that allowed them to exploit and receive visas for travel abroad. The Rom had heard that members of the ethnic German minority that had been living in Romania since the thirteenth century were receiving visas so they could visit or immigrate to Germany, their country of origin. Some Rom manufactured false identity papers saying they were ethnic Germans; some even learned to speak a little German. Those Rom granted visas went to Germany or Austria, where they were able to earn a better living.

In 1977 many Rom were so afraid of letting the authorities (particularly the state police, the Securitate) and *gaje* know they were Rom that only 230,000 officially declared themselves. Today there are an estimated 3 million to 3.5 million Rom in Romania, the largest concentration in any country in the world except for India, where 30 million to 35 million live.

In Romania there are thirteen distinct Rom tribes, more than in any other country in Europe.

The **Caldarari** make and fix copper drainage pipes.

Ciurari make strainers and other cooking utensils out of aluminum and wood (they also sell gold in Cluj).

Ursari were the bear tamers and entertainers; today they operate small businesses.

Zlátari make drainage pipes and metal containers from zinc.

Fierari (originally **Coāuaci**) worked as blacksmiths and repaired carriages; today they work repairing containers made from metal.

Lāutari are musicians.

Sitari make strainers, rolling pins, and other cooking utensils.

Cutitari sharpen cutlery, scissors, knives—anything with a metal blade.

Gábori buy and sell clothes and jewelry at fairs in Romania, Turkey, Hungary, and Germany, while a few still work at the more traditional job of making and repairing furnaces and hot water heaters.

Sfirnari were animal dealers and trainers (mostly horses) but today have small businesses.

Linguari make cutlery and rolling pins from wood.

Argintari are silversmiths.

Cortorari are still nomadic and basically survive by scavenging from garbage dumps and by petty thievery.

With renewed vigor xenophobic nationalism has swept Romania and has negatively affected the ethnic Hungarians, Jews, and particularly the Rom. Many have been spit at, called names, beaten by hooligans and skinheads, and burned out of their homes and villages. Every day hundreds of Rom leave Romania legally and illegally, hoping for a better future in Western Europe. Paradoxically, many of them have chosen to go to Germany, where they were persecuted under Hitler. But the benevolence of the German government and other European countries has worn thin, making the Rom one of many economic and political refugees to be sent back to their respective lands.

These are trying times for the Rom in Romania.

Cluj, Romania: A young Ciurari Rom girl at the Oşer market

Cluj, Romania *Carmen Şipoş* (age 29)

I was on the 3 P.M. train out of Budapest, which was scheduled to arrive in Cluj at midnight. I shared my train compartment with a Hungarian-Romanian young man who was a student in Budapest. He spoke fluent English.

The train arrived at the border at 7 P.M. The Romanian customs police rifled through my baggage hardly noticing my cameras, camera equipment, or film, but my violin, that was another matter.

"Is this your violin?" said the customs officer.

"Yes."

"Can you play it?"

"Why else would I be carrying it?"

"Prove it. Let me hear you play something."

I proceeded to take out the violin and play a Romanian folk melody, which brought several other passengers and customs police to our compartment.

"All right, that's enough. Give me the violin."

After inspecting the violin thoroughly, the officer handed it back to me. "Don't put it away just yet. Fill out these declaration papers so when you leave Romania we will know you are leaving with the same violin you brought in."

The market we visited today is called Oşer. Here people can come and sell whatever they want without a permit. Many Rom come and sell various goods they have brought back from Turkey. They have no problem crossing the Bulgarian and Turkish borders because they bribe the border guards with cigarettes, liquor, or money. The Rom we saw the most of today at the market were the Gábori. They are the best business negotiators. They had good jobs many years ago fixing pots, boilers, et cetera, and saved much of their money to purchase goods from abroad. They also became wealthy from the gold they passed down from generation to generation to generation. The Gábori women wear beautiful dresses and a lot of jewelry. They marry very young, between the ages of twelve and fifteen years old.

That man you met who squeezed your hand when you shook hands is from the Coāuaci tribe. This was the tribe my father-in-law came from. They usually lived in villages and were blacksmiths. Everyone in the village knew the blacksmith and respected him very much. He was the one who took care of their horses, the horses' shoes, wagons, carriages, and anything that was made of iron.

The Rom who still travel about Romania and who would travel throughout Europe if they could obtain visas are the Cortorari. They have no homes, no water to wash, they don't know about hospitals or school, and basically live like they did one hundred years ago, uncivilized. They unfortunately give other Rom a bad name and help perpetuate stereotypes of the dirty, stealing Rom.

My father was from the Lāutari, the musicians. He traveled outside of the country, participating in mar-

Cluj, Romania: Carmen Şipoş and her mother preparing dinner

riages, funerals, christenings, and concerts. He was worldly and was able to choose from what he saw as the best values and habits for his family. The Lāutari are clean, wear fine, elegant clothes, and are respected by the *gaje.* During the Ceauşescu regime the Lāutari were some of the few people, Romanian or Rom, who were given visas. From their travels they were able to tell their children what life was like in the other countries.

The Rom you see here in the streets of Cluj, the ones with tattoos all over their arms, are a group of Rom without any tribal name. They sell cigarettes, sunflower seeds, gum, and other little things in the streets. Sometimes the children are tattooed when they are very young so they don't feel it as much, just as we pierce a baby girl's ears when she is six to eight months old. When they become older, they are more aware of the pain and try to resist being tattooed or having pierced ears.

In the villages where the Rom and *gaje* live in close proximity to each other there are more bias-related problems against the Rom. But in the city where there are so many people most *gaje* don't bother the Rom. Sometimes you do hear a *gajo* yell at a Rom, "chara," which is the name for the crow. *Chara* is meant to be a dark-skinned person who steals silver and gold. And the crow is black and often steals shiny objects for his nest. When we get angry at a *gajo*, we call him "mokan," which means mountain person. Many Romanians come from the villages in the mountains, and even after twenty years of living in the city they still smell and act like their farm animals. They are *mokan* to us.

In Romania there are no special schools for the Rom. Perhaps if we had these schools, with good teachers, we could teach a generation of Rom youth the importance of reading and writing. Without a good education for all the Rom here in Romania we will remain primitive and receive less respect from the *gaje*. I want my daughter to finish high school and go on to college so she can have a better life than I have.

I am not ashamed of being a Rom. I love the music, dance, song, language, cuisine, and folklore, but if we want to advance as a people, like the Jews, we have to better educate ourselves and not just live by our "street smarts." We also have to change our attitude and philosophy that say, In my house don't steal, and act as a civilized human, but what you do somewhere else I don't care. This is a selfish, individualistic way of life that too often characterizes the Rom way of life.

In school we learned about the Romanian Jewish tragedy that took place during World War II, but nothing about the Rom experience. My mother and father each had aunts and uncles that were forcibly taken to concentration camps in Transnistria, where they died from disease. My husband's great-uncle and great-grandfather were sent to concentration camps in Poland and never returned. All Rom, educated and uneducated, know about these horrible experiences of World War II, and I feel it could happen again. Look what is happening now in Germany—the skinheads are attacking all foreigners and the government has responded by deporting all of the Rom refugees. The skinheads are even attacking the Jews and their institutions throughout Europe. But the Jews are better organized than we are. They will be able to combat this neo-Nazism. We fight among ourselves too often and hardly are able to come together without a deluge of arguments when we have Rom congresses. Here in Romania the Rom have had a tragic history even before World War II. For nearly four hundred years, until the mid-nineteenth century, we were slaves bought and sold just like the blacks were in the United States. How come I know about the black American slave experience and they and the rest of the *gaje* in the United States don't know anything about our horrendous years of slavery?

After a few minutes the customs policeman returned and read the papers, stamped them, and said, "Very well, give me the violin and I will stamp it so we can identify it when you leave the country."

"Stamp it! Are you crazy! This violin is one hundred and twelve years old, you'll ruin it!" And I grabbed my violin back.

Finally, after a lengthy discussion in Romanian with my new friend, the customs policeman left the train, throwing the declaration papers onto the floor.

Welcome to Romania, I thought. Some things take years to change.

TOP LEFT
Cluj, Romania: A young Cortorari Rom
boy begging for money with his baby brother
BOTTOM LEFT
Cluj, Romania: Adi Şipoş in a neighbor's home typically
decorated in a Romanes style.
RIGHT
Cluj, Romania: Andra Şipoş standing in front of the Rom Union
headquarters

23

Cluj, Romania   *Iancu Burta* (age 15)

Upon arriving in Cluj, I took a taxi to the home of Carmen Şipoş, a Rom woman who was told by a mutual friend in Budapest that I was coming. Despite it being midnight Carmen and her husband, Adi, welcomed me with immense hospitality.

Carmen's father had been known by all as the greatest Rom violinist in Transylvania, a fact that Carmen was extremely proud of. It gave her a certain amount of status in the community. Upstairs sleeping in two large rooms were Carmen's mother, daughter, niece, and older brother.

We talked and talked until 4:00 A.M, when we were served a snack. Finally I closed my weary eyes at 4:30 A.M. and fell fast asleep.

Little did I know I would barely sleep while in Cluj. Eating, drinking, talking, singing, dancing, and more eating through the early morning hours was my regimen for the next two weeks. It is the Rom way.

We travel to Germany every three months, selling things we brought with us from Romania. We then buy a few things that are difficult to find here, return to Cluj, and change our deutsch marks into Romanian lei but for a larger amount than the banks officially give you. Then we buy and sell here and begin our journey back to Germany after three months. I enjoy this work because I meet many different people, travel, and see places I've never seen before. If I had to work in a job where I came every day precisely at 8 A.M. and left precisely at 5 P.M., same people, same scenery, I would die from boredom. That is why I left school at age thirteen. I was bored with learning things I would never need or use in my life. But I can read and write and in my spare time I read the Bible and adventure stories.

Probably when some people read my interview they will think—He can't be very smart, he left school at the age of thirteen. Look how he and his mother dress, they must be primitive people. And I would answer those people in America like this: First of all just because I don't sit in a chair in front of a blackboard with thirty other students doesn't mean I can't learn. I know more about the geography of Romania, Hungary, Austria, and Germany than most *gaje* adults. My father has taught me how to repair cars, pots, pans, furnaces, any metal containers, and sharpen knives. He does these kinds of jobs while we travel back and forth between Germany and Romania. How many *gaje* in America my age speak three languages, understand the business of exchanging foreign currencies, and know a lot about various European cultures? Schools are good for you when you are very young and just beginning to learn about the world. But after you know how to read, write, add, subtract, multi-

Cluj, Romania: Iancu and his mother, Gábori Rom, counting their money after a good day of business in Oşer

ply, and divide, I think you can learn more from being out in the real world. My mother and father are my teachers now.

When I'm not working, I'm listening to music and watching videos. I like to listen to heavy metal, rap, and Rom music. My favorite band is Motorhead and my favorite movies are the Jean Claude Van Damme and Chuck Norris films—lots of action. I would like to meet them and ask how long they studied martial arts. If I did a sport, it would be either judo or karate.

Cluj, Romania   *Coca Jonica Radu* (age 42)

This necklace I am wearing which is intertwined with my hair is called *bişaria*. All these coins are authentic, very old, and from all over the world. When the *bişaria* is made from only gold coins, then it is called *salbādegalben*, or just *galbi*. I never take this out of my hair, sleeping and and washing my hair with it. When I become old and will prepare for my death, putting out new clothes on my bed to wear and having a fancy dinner prepared, I will then take the *bişaria* out of my hair and give it to my only daughter. She in turn will give it to her oldest daughter when she prepares to die. This *bişaria* was given to my great-great-great-grandmother after she was released from being a slave in 1851. The *bişaria* is a sign of wealth and prestige, especially if you have a *galbi*. The tradition

LEFT
Cluj, Romania: Gheorghe and his wife, Coca Jonica, at the Oşer market
BELOW
Cluj, Romania: Market day in Oşer

also served a useful purpose for carrying one's own jewelry. Since we were wanderers, never knowing when the *gaje* would chase us from our campsite, we had to be able to escape quickly, so we wore all of our jewelry on our bodies—rings, necklaces, pins, and bracelets. We didn't hide it in some box like the *gaje*. Buying a fancy piece of jewelry and only wearing it a few times a year seems ridiculous to me. Who can appreciate the beauty and prestige when the ring or bracelet is kept in the dark?

Cluj, Romania *Gheorghe Radu* (age 47)

I have lived my whole life in Tîrgu-Jiu. I belong to the Zlátari Rom, which means most of the men work by making and repairing drainage pipes and other things made of zinc and other metals. We don't come often to the market here in Oşer. When we do it is to buy some clothes or shoes. This time, however, we came because my daughter became quite ill, having drank some poison by mistake. She was taken to the hospital, which is expensive. I'm trying to sell some leather belts I made to get enough money to pay her hospital bills.

I know many Rom who left Tîrgu-Jiu and went to Germany. The economic situation here is not good and it doesn't seem to be getting any better. Some of the *gaje*, especially in the National Democratic party, have loudly let their dislike for us be known. I work and live among the *gaje* but there is a kind of a silent understanding between them and us that we don't trust each other. Unfortunately there are some Rom, particularly the Cortorari, who really still travel from city to city just begging and stealing. They give a bad name to the rest of the Rom. It is difficult to find work, and these Rom don't

Cluj, Romania: A Linguari Rom selling his wooden wares

Cluj, Romania: An impromptu concert on a street corner

want to change and educate their children. Still I don't think the Rom who are in refugee camps in Germany should be forced to return to Romania. Why aren't they forcing the *gaje* who have entered Germany from other countries like Russia back to their homelands?

Gilău, Romania *Mindra* (age 13)

I was born in a village not far from here, moving to Gilău when I was two years old. We are one of only three Gábori Rom families in the whole town. My family is poor. We are eight children and my father's job fixing furnaces and making water heaters doesn't pay that much. Now that I am married, my husband's family is responsible for feeding me and my baby. My husband is fifteen years old and does some selling and repairing of furnaces and bathtubs. I quit school when I was twelve. I can read and write a little, but now my day is occupied taking care of my baby. We get along with most of the *gaje* here. We must, Gilău is so small. But I know of other places where some Rom have been beaten. The economy is terrible and the rise of nationalism among the *gaje* has resulted in an atmosphere of prejudice. In our home we only speak Romani, but in the streets Romanian with the *gaje*. Maybe after my children will all be in school in eight to ten years I will sew and design dresses like the one I'm wearing now. When I go to Cluj many tourists stop me on the street and ask me about my dress and where they can buy one like it. Maybe I can have a boutique selling Rom fashions.

Gilău, Romania: Petru, a Gábori Rom woman

RIGHT
Gilău, Romania: Mindra and her baby

30

Cluj, Romania: Rom children playing in their neighborhood

Šukar Lujlujdij
(Beautiful Flower)

Romanian Lāutari Rom

Transcribed by Karen Elaine
as sung by Irina Koszta

Sung not in strict rhythm. Adagio

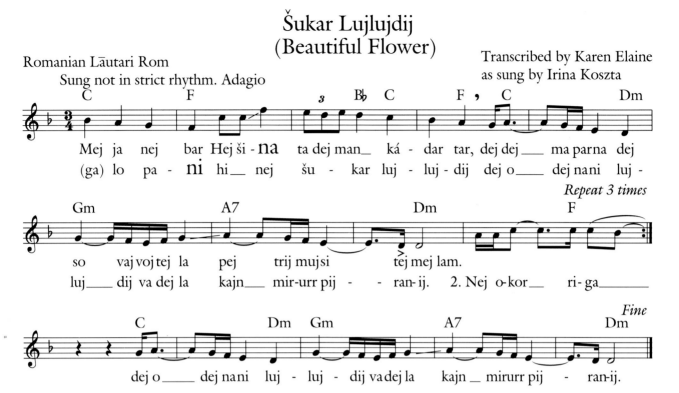

Mej ja nej bar Hej ši - na ta dej man__ ká - dar tar, dej dej__ ma parna dej
(ga) lo pa - ni hi__ nej šu - kar luj - luj - dij dej o___ dej nani luj -

so vaj voj tej la pej trij mujsi tej mej lam.
luj___ dij va dej la kajn___ mir-urr pij - - ran-ij. 2. Nej o-kor__ ri - ga_____

dej o ___ dej nani luj - luj - dij vadej la kajn __ mirurr pij - ran-ij.

Hey, hey, come with me, my beauty.
Hey, šina, give yourself to me.
Come, because I want to die.
Don't give me any pillow to sleep
on because I want to die with my
head under your arms.
On the other side of the river
there is a beautiful flower growing.
Ten thousand times I want
to kiss you because you
smell so good, like the flower
in the garden.

Nagykálló, Hungary: On the road to Nyíregyháza

HUNGARY

The earliest written mention of the Rom in Hungary can be traced to 1417, prior to the invasion of the Ottoman Turks. Skilled in crafts that were in demand, the Rom were later welcomed to Hungary by King Mathias Cornius (1458–1490). One of their first settlements was near the town of Sibiu, which today is in Transylvania, Romania.

In parts of southeastern Hungary the Rom were forced into slavery beginning at the end of the fifteenth century. At this time and for many years to come, the Hungarian Rom were blamed for the most abominable crimes: kidnapping children, rape, and cannibalism. Most of all, the Rom feared the accusation of cannibalism. From the late eighteenth century through World War I, the peasantry of Central Europe were extremely influenced by the growing number of oral and written stories about vampires. The Rom were associated with these stories and were rumored to kill (often by impaling their victims) and then eat their prey. Those accused were either beaten or hanged.

Maria Theresa (1740–1780), queen of Hungary and Bohemia, tried to "civilize" the Rom by making them more acceptable to the general public. She prohibited the Rom from sleeping in tents, working in their traditional occupations, electing their own chiefs, speaking Romani, traveling from camp to camp, and marrying if they did not have the means to support a family. The men were forced into the military and the children coerced to attend schools. These edicts, clothed in the cloak of gossamer liberalism, were actually part of a plan to destroy the Rom culture. The policies of Maria Theresa and her successor, her son Joseph II (1780–1790), brought pain and hardship to thousands of Rom.

Many Rom committed suicide when their children were taken away from them and put into special boarding schools. Others remained nomadic and moved into the forests. Out of necessity some Rom became skilled thieves. Those Rom caught either not sending their children to school and/or stealing were hanged, tortured, or beheaded.

Because of the strict laws against vagrancy during the reigns of Maria Theresa and Joseph II, nomadism among the Hungarian Rom was greatly reduced. By the end of the nineteenth century it had come to a complete end.

In the period between World War I and World War II, the Rom in Hungary survived as best they could. Some Rom owned and farmed land. Others gathered natural resources (wood, clay, straw, grass) or collected junk to make mats, clothespins, knives, tools, scrubbing boards, utensils, flutes, and so forth for sale and barter.

In 1943 the Rom in Hungarian-occupied Transylvania and Carpathian-Ukraine were deported to several concentration camps, where most were murdered. Some Rom within Hungary, particularly those from the southeastern part of the country, were also deported to labor and death camps. Luckily, most of the Rom in this area were saved by the fast-advancing Soviet army, which had overrun two-thirds of Hungary, just reaching the outskirts of Budapest by November 1944.

After World War II the Hungarian government attempted to turn all private farms into collectives, making those Rom who were not farmers into laborers. The Rom resisted the Communist government's policy of assimilation by escaping from their jobs, sabotaging their work, and purposely slowing down on the job site. Finally, the government realized the futility of trying to forcibly integrate the Rom.

During the years of Communist rule of Hungary, there was no iron curtain for the Rom. Budapest was a city that attracted travelers and traders from as far south as Istanbul, and it was near Vienna in the "free" West. Thus, the city became the crossroads for a kind of underground railroad. Rom with documents and visas would ferry across the different borders, conducting their business. The Rom were able to buy relatively inexpensive gold in Istanbul, then smuggle it across the borders through Hungary to Austria, where they were able to sell it at a profit for Western "hard" currencies like Austrian shillings, German marks, or American dollars. Then they would return to their respective villages in Hungary and purchase many luxury items with their earnings. Many Rom throughout the former Eastern Bloc set out on this arduous trek. Some, of course, were caught and given fines and/or imprisoned.

Today there are about 600,000 to 800,000 Rom living in Hungary. The main tribes are the Romungro, Vlahura, and Olach. There are two elected Rom representatives in the Hungarian parliament, Aladár Howáth and Zoltán Csorba, who are trying to raise the standard of living for the Rom and the level of consciousness and acceptance among the *gaje*. A major problem facing the Hungarian Rom today is the rise of nationalism, which is being championed by the Democratic Forum, the governing party. Their rhetoric espouses the exclusive right of the "true Hungarians" to have a voice in the new Hungary.

Budapest, Hungary: On the main stage, Rom youth dancing with energy and excitement at the Hungarian Rom festival

This attitude clearly excludes a significant portion of the Hungarian population who are Jews, Romanians, and Rom. As a result the police will all too often ignore bias attacks against the Rom by skinheads and other right-wing political groups. This lack of empathy and tacit approval by some of the authorities and general public have created an atmosphere of frustration, depression, and wariness among the Rom.

Budapest, Hungary: Irene Németh and her friend enjoying a summer day

Budapest, Hungary *Irene Németh* (age 12)

I began learning to speak English only last year. When I listen to rap music, watch MTV, or see some American movies, I listen very carefully to the English. Unfortunately I don't speak Romani, but I can understand some of it. Many Rom children my age don't know the language because their parents didn't speak it at home. But I do know the music and folktales of the Hungarian Rom. I learned them from my grandmother, whose mother came from Turkey.

Of all the famous singers today I like Michael Jackson, George Michael, and Madonna, but I think she acts like a whore. A woman shouldn't be so sexual in public. What you do in private is your business.

When you say "Hungary" to a tourist, he usually thinks of Hungarian Rom, their music and dance. What would the Hungarian culture be without any Rom? Probably quite boring. We are only 5 percent of the country's population but we influence nearly 90 percent of all the folk music. Our music is the national music and we perform it with deep feeling, better than any *gajo*. It seems pretty stupid when you think about how many Hungarians dislike us because we are different. Who plays in the fancy hotels and restaurants all over the country—the *gaje*? I guess every country in the world has some minority in its land they need to be angry with and jealous of. It wouldn't be natural to look at oneself to see if you might be the cause of the problem.

Arriving in Budapest was like returning to an old friend I remembered so well. Having previously done research in Budapest, I was familiar with the city and its Rom and Jewish neighborhoods.

After a good night's sleep I ventured into the Rom world. I chose to walk to most of my destinations. Traversing through Budapest, with its narrow streets, hidden alleyways, quaint shops, neighborhood parks, and the beautiful Danube River separating the city into two distinct parts (Buda and Pest), I never knew what new charm I would encounter around the next corner.

My first destination was the old Jewish neighborhood, because I knew there were Rom who had moved in there after World War II. Just past the orthodox synagogue in a park on Klauzal Square were several groups of Rom children playing. I slowly approached and took my camera out and began to take photographs. This attracted the attention of a lovely Rom girl named Irene, who spoke some English. After introducing myself and explaining the nature of my work, I was quickly surrounded by a dozen curious Rom children, all asking questions of me at the same time. Who was my favorite rock-and-roll musician? Who was my favorite NBA player? Did I ever meet Eddie Murphy or Arnold Schwarzenegger on the streets of New York City?

Budapest, Hungary   *Sándor "Buffo" Rigo* (age 38)

Budapest, Hungary: Sándor Rigo and his wife, Maria

My name is Sándor Rigo, but everyone knows me by my nickname, Buffo. The name comes from opera. When the tenor sings the high C a little false, we say he made a buffo. He is a comic character, always joking, something my father saw in me when I was young. I was born in Szombathely, a few kilometers from the Austrian border. My father was a violinist and he began teaching me at eight years old, a late beginner. An excellent violinist, he could read music—so he taught me how to read as well. Most of the time now when I play the violin, it is without music. We Rom have a very special gift and that is being able to learn difficult music only by ear. When I play classical, I usually read music, however, once I was playing at a party outside and the wind blew over my music stand, scattering all the music. Luckily I knew the piece and just kept on playing. My two oldest sons play instruments, too. The oldest, who is twenty-one years old, plays the violin and the twenty-year-old plays the cymbalom. For us it is a tradition that the males in the family follow in their father's footsteps as musicians. For the women it is another tradition.

My wife's father in my opinion was the best Hungarian violinist. His name was Sándor Jaroka. He was crowned the king of Rom violin music by the Rom in Detroit, Cleveland, and Chicago. Consequently, my wife has music in her blood, the talent and ear for music. She is able to play something from any instrument she picks up. But because she is a woman, her main responsibility is to the home, where she takes care of the children. But even this tradition is gradually changing because I know of a few married women who play in Rom orchestras with their husbands and sometimes children.

In Hungary you have to make a distinction among the different Rom tribes. We are the Rom with the tribal name Romungro, and we generally are musicians. We don't speak Romani well because we were urbanized three to four generations back. We settled in houses, didn't travel, and worked for and among the *gaje*. Then there are the Olach Rom, a tribe that came originally from Transylvania. They are businesspeople, buying and selling mostly antiques at one time, but different items today. The third group we just call Cigan (Rom in Hungarian). They are laborers. They work in the factories, in construction, or on farms. Of these three groups, we Romungro have a little higher social status because we have traveled the world and are generally better educated. Many of the Olach and Cigan Rom say we are not Rom but *gaje*. I feel bad when they say this to me. Even though I have more contact with the *gaje* and I don't speak Romani doesn't mean I'm not a Rom. I'm sad that I don't

Budapest, Hungary: A young Romungro Rom following in the musical heritage of his father and grandfather

Hodász, Hungary: An Olach Rom musician, holding the violin folkstyle

speak the language, but it is not my fault, blame my great-great-great-grandfather who settled in some village.

We have had many problems here between the government and the Rom. They want to help us but they want to do it in their own way without really knowing who we are and what our culture is all about. You have to know the people before you can dictate to them. In America twenty, thirty years ago there were many problems between the black people and white society. Some of the biggest problems came from the fact that the white people, the administrators, the judicial system, schools, et cetera, tried to turn the blacks into white people. You can't do this, it's impossible! Here in Hungary we have had the same problem. You can't change or make a Rom into something he isn't. Assimilation will never work and only creates extreme tensions between the Rom and the *gaje*. Rom like to come together after working all day to visit, eat, sing, and dance in the evening. But for the *gaje* they look at this as if we are uncouth and only know how to party. Do we have to be quiet and subdued in our homes like the *gaje*? After a long day at work we like to socialize with our friends and family. We enjoy celebrating just for the sake of celebration, and not waiting for a holiday or formal party to sing, dance, or play music.

The Rom do have the opportunity to study and become lawyers, scientists, even astronauts, but in reality it doesn't happen much. I do know some Rom who are doctors, lawyers, and teachers, but most Rom don't have the force, the drive, to become so educated. To aspire to become such a professional you have to fight and persist. Perhaps if we had schools just for the Rom, like the Jewish private schools here in Budapest, we could begin to educate a new generation of children that would see there is a whole world of various opportunities out there.

Budapest, Hungary: Performing on a traditional Rom percussive instrument, the milk can

Every day I would spend some hours at the park taking photographs, interviewing the children, playing Ping-Pong, and giving out chewing gum. At the park I noticed that it was the Rom girls who took care of their younger siblings, while the older boys played Ping-Pong, card games (rummy) for money, or just sat around talking and smoking. Both the boys and girls were fascinated with my cameras, constantly asking me to let them take some pictures. My own picture was taken many times.

Another problem is the growth of racism here in Hungary. Now that we are a democracy, one can say anything, any expletive, any negative word against another group of people without repercussions from the police. Consequently many of the Rom who are poor or have no work feel no remorse when they steal food, clothes, et cetera. They reason that if a *gajo* can be outside of the law and the police just ignore his repugnant behavior, then I can be outside of the law as well. I don't know which came first, the Rom's antisocial behavior in terms of stealing or the *gaje*'s suspicion and prejudice of us. Sometimes my children have encountered some name-calling—like being called a dirty Rom by a *gajo*. I've told my children to look and see what expression his face has and know you have nice clothes, a beautiful home, and bathe every day; and realize he's dirtier than you.

I am proud to be a Rom. Some people are very jealous of my musical abilities and believe I live a romantic, bohemian life. Let them keep on thinking this! Everyone's life has two sides. But I hope we can change some of our ways that I feel hold us back from advancing as a people. Sometimes we try to show our strength and solidarity too often with physical brute force, instead of intelligence and cleverness. We have a Rom proverb that says: "More with intelligence than with power." I hope more of us learn to live by this motto in the future.

Budapest, Hungary: Rom children at Klauzal Square Park on a summer day

Budapest, Hungary *Istvan Doci* (age 16)

I am a Rom. This means I live life to its fullest. For me, pleasing someone, whether *gajo* or Rom, through song, dance, and music gives me the greatest satisfaction. How would our world be without music, with only the deafening sounds from machines and the wails of pain of millions of troubled people? Music perhaps isn't a cure for our problems, but it can help people to momentarily enjoy and appreciate their lives a little more. I like different kinds of music—reggae, disco, jazz, and classical, but Rom music pierces my heart like no other music can. Without Rom music and poetry Hungarian culture would be rather simple. How many tourists would stay as long as they do in Budapest if there wasn't any Rom music? Perhaps our music, with its intense sounds and wild rhythms, reflects our wanderings. Rom people should never feel ashamed, whether they are poor or rich. We come from India, a land that has influenced the whole world. What is English but an Indo-European language? I bet most Americans don't even realize the influence of Sanskrit or Hindi on the English language.

Budapest, Hungary: Istvan Doci in Klauzal Square Park

Budapest, Hungary: A Rom youth ensemble, dressed in their traditional clothes, performing at the Hungarian Rom festival

Budapest, Hungary *Monika Sztolyba* (age 14)

Before I left Budapest many of the boys warned me to be careful. "The Rom near Nyíregyháza are much poorer than we are." "They will be sympathetic with you in the beginning, catch you off guard, stab you with a knife, and steal all your belongings." "You see, the Rom of rural Hungary look upon any *gajo* with great suspicion and fear."

During my travels I found that often the Rom in the city were a bit prejudiced against their brethren in the country. They felt they had become more sophisticated, learning how to live with the *gaje*, while the country Rom were more primitive, having only the farmers and peasants to learn from. In the villages in eastern Hungary and the Carpathian Mountains I found this rarely to be true.

During the summer I come to the park almost every day except when I go to the pool or visit my relatives in Mátészalka. Most of my friends are Rom, though I have a few Hungarian friends. I would probably have more *gajo* friends but their parents don't like their children playing with Rom children. They are afraid we will teach them something bad because many of us are "primitive" [laughter].

I like school, especially my science class. I read a lot of science fiction in my spare time. Unfortunately we don't learn anything about our culture in the schools. That is why the *gaje* are ignorant about us. It would be hard to find a teacher who knew enough about the Rom, unless of course they were Rom themselves. Just like there are *gaje* that are dishonest, I must admit there are some Rom who are dishonest, lazy, and do some stealing. Every society has their hooligans. But the *gajo* looks at us a bit warily because our skin is darker, we speak a different language, and have diverse customs. Whenever a Rom walks into a room or building with a bunch of *gaje*, immediately the eyes of suspicion are upon him. This is something I will have to live with for the rest of my life.

I saw the movie *Home Alone*. It was great. I bet it is a lot of fun being an actor in Hollywood. I thought about being an actress but I'm not sure, maybe a scientist instead. Mixing those chemicals and trying to come up with some new medicines for a disease is really challenging. Once in our science lab my friend and I were mixing some chemicals when the beaker we were heating exploded all over the class. Luckily no one got hurt but our teacher was a bit upset. Wouldn't it be great if I became the first Rom woman in the world to win a Nobel Prize in science? Don't be so sure I won't do it.

Budapest, Hungary: Monika Sztolyba and her friend Doci

Budapest, Hungary *Tivados Foityol* (age 42)

Budapest, Hungary: Tivados Foityol at home

I was born in Makó, in southern Hungary, not far from Szeged. I come from a family of musicians. There is a book, a very old book, that mentions my great-great-grandfather, who was the most famous Rom violinist of his time throughout Transylvania. He originally came from Oradea, Romania. I belong to the sect of Rom known as the Romungro. The Romungro are mostly musicians here in Hungary, while the other large group, the Olach, are working mostly with their hands. Many of the Romungro, like our family, worked so much for the Hungarians, playing music in their homes, restaurants, and at their parties, we forgot much of our Romani language. We became assimilated, dressing like the Hungarian gentry in elegant clothes so we would be more readily accepted.

Though the Communist era has finally come to an end, in our new so-called democracy the Rom are encountering more problems from the Hungarians now than ever before. Democracy has brought the right for everyone to freely speak his mind—freedom of speech—and many are doing exactly that. The Jews and the Rom have become the black sheep for the Hungarians once again. If there is something wrong with our economy, schools, or crime, the Rom are to blame since we are known to be "thieves" and "liars" [laughter]. There have been Rom burned out of their homes in the countryside while the police look the other way. We are waiting for our own Los Angeles riots.

I have a band that consists of violin, viola, cymbalom, bass, and clarinet, playing any kind of music. Hungarian Rom are the best musicians among the Rom in the world, not Romanians, Bulgarians, or even Russians. My band

Budapest, Hungary: Tivados introducing the next guest artist during the Hungarian Rom festival

traveled throughout Europe playing not only Hungarian Rom music but Spanish, English, French, German, Jewish, Arabic, Turkish, and opera music. We recently came back from a four-month stint in Djakarta, Indonesia, where we played all of the above kinds of music plus Japanese and Vietnamese music as well. I would say that of all the kinds of music we play, Jewish is the closest to Rom. The scales, harmonies, and stylization all have some Rom similarities. The cymbalom that is so popular among the Rom musicians here in Hungary and in Romania came from the Jews. The Jews brought the instrument as they wandered from the East to Europe. We even say among ourselves that he or she is playing the Jewish-style cymbalom because of the particular tuning and harmonies.

Budapest, Hungary *Tibor "Tibi" Olöh* (age 18)

I finished school in June, now I'm on vacation. I come to the park to meet my friends. We play billiards, cards, talk—just hang out. Everyone is just themselves. We don't try to act unfriendly but we tend to stay with only Rom. District 7 used to be the Jewish quarter before the war, now more and more Rom are moving in.

My father is a well-known cymbalom player, performing in the Panorama Hotel, and is active in local politics. He gets paid well and receives good tips from the tourists that stay at the hotel. My brother, who plays the violin, sometimes plays with him. I play the guitar but not professionally. I plan to go to hotel school, where I will learn about the tourist business. Working as a manager of a large, expensive hotel like the Gellért in Buda would be exciting, especially because you meet people from all over the world.

Though I am eighteen, I don't plan to get married until twenty-five or twenty-seven. It was the tradition of my father's generation when the men married at age fifteen, sixteen, and seventeen. Some still do but more Rom boys are waiting until they are a little older. One reason is that when you marry so young you have to live with your parents. What kind of job is a fifteen-year-old going to have? More of us are finishing high school, so the boys wait until the age of eighteen or nineteen before they think about marriage. Here, unlike in other countries, the Rom men choose their own wives. We don't have arranged marriages, that is old-fashioned, and before I marry I would like to travel. It is not as easy to travel with a wife and children. When we get married, we don't wait long to begin a family.

LEFT
Budapest, Hungary: Tibor Olöh playing a game of gin rummy Sunday afternoon in Klauzal Square Park
BELOW
Budapest, Hungary: A high school in Pest that is attended by many Rom

As the largest minority in Hungary we have made little progress these last three years since the end of communism. If anything, some things have become worse. There are a lot more incidents where skinheads have attacked Rom here in Budapest. The police can be nearby and they just look the other way. One Rom girl was taken to an abandoned house and raped by four skinheads. That girl will never receive justice and now she feels shameful among the Rom because she lost her virginity before she married. If we catch those guys, we won't take them to the police but mete out ourselves a just punishment for the crime. Look what is happening with the Rom in Germany. They are being forced back to Romania. Romania is no place to live, especially if you are Hungarian or Rom. Nothing more but some articles have been written about what is happening with the Rom refugees in Germany. Perhaps it is our fault. We should organize and demonstrate in front of the German Embassy here in Budapest. But that is one of our greatest problems, we can't seem to organize ourselves to fight for our rights. Too often it is done only by a few Rom leaders like those in the Parliament. Organizing is something we could learn from the Jews, fighting for our brothers wherever they may be in the world.

From Budapest I traveled east to Nyíregyháza. Upon arrival I immediately took the streetcar to the tourist office, where one could book sleeping accommodations in a private house. Unfortunately they had just closed and the lady behind the desk, who was busy doing her nails, didn't seem eager to help me.

"We are closed, closed, come back tomorrow."

"I know you just closed but I need a place to sleep tonight."

Finally she told me of a cheap hotel that was occupied by only Poles, Ukrainians, and Russians. Some of them were on vacation but most were living there while buying and selling various wares. Hungary was a shopper's paradise for the Ukrainians and Russians since there was a shortage of everything in their countries.

After stowing my gear in my room, I decided to see if I could remember where my friend András lived. He was the one and only person I knew in Nyíregyháza who could direct me to the Rom neighborhoods and help me with translating. I had lost his address and hadn't seen him in five years. But my memory didn't fail me and I found his home.

TOP LEFT
Nyíregyháza, Hungary: Anti-Rom graffiti on a wall in the former Jewish quarter
BOTTOM LEFT
Nyíregyháza, Hungary: Anti-Rom graffiti has become more prevalent since the collapse of communism. This reads: YOU ARE A DOG! WE ARE THE GYPSY BEATERS!

Hodász, Hungary: Grandmother and granddaughter listening to Pastor Sáni's sermon

The next day we drove to the small town of Hodász. When we arrived in the Rom neighborhood, we immediately felt the stares of curiosity from those in the streets. First, we were the only *gaje* around, and secondly, we were driving a new Mercedes. I saw a group of Rom men working at a construction site and walked over, introducing myself. I met Sándor Rézmüves, who explained to me that they were building a church.

Hodász, Hungary: Immediately after early evening church service, impromptu Rom dances take place.

Hodász, Hungary: Pastor Sáni enjoying the music and dance with his congregants

Hodász, Hungary   *Pastor Sáni* (age 35)

Today our new democracy guarantees that all Rom children can learn about their own history in their mother tongue. Our history begins in India about one thousand years ago. When the Rom were forced out of their homeland, they began to wander and split into several groups. We are descendants of these wandering folk. It was difficult to keep up the language and culture because wherever they went they were an oppressed people. Nevertheless they always resisted assimilation. Today we cannot say the Rom are wandering. Most Rom, particularly here in Hungary, have a legal residence, though some may travel by caravan searching for business. However, many Rom men have moved to Budapest, where they work in the building industry. This was a big, big mistake. Rom were always free-spirited people, but to find a job they had to leave their families for faraway places. As a result the mother tongue and cultured weakened.

We used to follow the custom which began in India of the one-person tribunal, the *vadja*. The *vadja* was a man who everyone respected and paid attention to. He was similar to a judge; if he gave an order it was executed. The *vadja* was the law and the leader of a Rom *kumpania* [a company of Rom that traveled together]. He punished and rewarded people according to his judgment. To become a *vadja* one had to be a well-respected man. It was knowledge, reputation, and behavior that were the criteria for being chosen. When he was chosen, there was a ceremony which took place granting him this authority. He had to wear black leather pants and a coat, a sign indicating to Rom outside the *kumpania* he was the *vadja*. In Hodász this tradition came to an end in the early 1960s, but there were some other communities in Hungary where even in the 1980s there was a *vadja*. As far as I know, there are still some Rom communities that have a *vadja*. Today we don't accept this. The law of the land and our belief in God rule us now.

Until recently a minority couldn't organize itself. It couldn't maintain its distinct culture, speak its mother tongue, and use its traditional skills to make a living. During the last forty years Hungarian Rom were ruled by laws made by Hungarians which encouraged us to assimilate. But deep in their hearts the Rom always maintained their unique identity and secretly organized themselves while being suppressed. One positive point about those forty years was we had jobs. Once people had jobs there was bread on the table. Now the problem is there is no work, consequently there is not enough bread. But we can organize, speak and write our language, and participate in the legal process. Now we are truly liberated.

Hodász, Hungary: Antique Greek Orthodox iconography hanging in the Rom church

Hodász, Hungary *Sándor Rézmüves* (age 58)

Sándor invited us to come back that afternoon at 5 P.M., when I would have the opportunity to meet and take photographs of Rom children. They would be attending church services.

After the church services two guitarists and a vocalist began an impromptu concert. Instantly a circle of Rom and various dancers, young and old, took to the floor, moving to the pulsating music. It was an incredible sight. The music, dancing, singing, and overall joy were so magnetic I gave András my cameras and joined the dancers. My dancing in my shorts and heavy work boots gave good reason for everyone to laugh. Eventually I took my violin out and joined the musicians. This created another stir, a *gajo* playing their music. The concert lasted three hours with two Jews and two hundred Rom enjoying the beauty and spontaneity of one another's friendship.

I am the chapel manager helping to coordinate the construction of our new Greek-Catholic church. The chapel which we are sitting in now was built out of clay and pure mud. It was bought by our grandfathers and fathers over fifty years ago. My grandfather, father, and other fathers would go begging for food, eggs, flour, sugar, et cetera, and bring it to the priest Miklos Solyon. He would then sell this food and use the money toward buying the little house. When he purchased this place, Solyon used it as a school, since the law under the Communists forbade churches. We would go there with our priest as if to learn, but in secret we were observing mass there. Miklos Solyon even wrote the ABCs on the walls to make it look like a school. He wasn't Rom, but we loved him very much. These days our chapel is damaged and too small. God helped us and we were able to build the new foundation. Unfortunately we ran out of money. As the chapel manager I would like to ask the other Rom in the world to support us so we have a place to pray and observe mass.

In the years just before World War I, my grandfather and father came to Hodász from Transylvania. Altogether there were about five or six families that settled here. In those times my grandfather was able to make a decent living doing a little farming and repairing pots, pans, wagon wheels, and other things like that for the *gaje*. Now there are six hundred eighty Rom living here, Olach and Hungarian Rom. I am Olach and speak the Olach dialect. Since the Hungarian Rom don't speak the language, we don't have much to do with them. There are no problems between us. We say good morning to each other but we live our separate lives.

ABOVE
Hodász, Hungary: Sándor Rézmüves
TOP RIGHT
Hodász, Hungary: A Rom mother and her children
BOTTOM RIGHT
Hodász, Hungary: The Rom Greek Orthodox church

The times are much worse now economically than they were during the time of my grandfather. There are no job opportunities. No opportunity to farm because it is still the collective cooperative farms that are operating here. The new government didn't give us our land back and only God knows who will get what later. The poor families who are unemployed and have children get fifty-eight dollars a week, an awfully small amount. For a family with five or six people the money runs out before the next unemployment check comes. At the end of the week there is no money to buy bread or milk.

When I was a young boy, I remember the Jews of the community well. When they had this holiday on Saturday [the Sabbath], they didn't work, so it was the Rom who worked for them, lighting a fire and bringing them their food. I worked in a soda factory owned by a Jew named Fuchs. All the workers were Rom, no Hungarians. We carried the water and filled the bottles with carbonation. We had a very good relationship with the Jews. My mother used to clean, cook, and do the laundry at several Jewish homes. She knew about their special dietary laws and would cook *lećso* and cholent with beans on Friday nights. If a woman wanted to take the cholent to a friend's or relative's home, it was my father or mother who carried the cholent, because the Jews couldn't carry anything after sundown on Fridays. In 1944 the Germans came and gathered all the Jews of the town into their temple. It was spring and most of those deported never came back. We were gathered to be put on trains in late December 1944, but the Russians were quickly approaching. The Germans were afraid and ran away. They had no time to finish their job and that is how we survived.

During the time of my youth a Rom wedding looked

TOP LEFT
Hodász, Hungary: Some of the matriarchs of the Rom community
TOP RIGHT
Hodász, Hungary: Rom father and child standing in front of the newly built church foundation
LEFT BOTTOM
Hodász, Hungary: After church services, an impromptu Rom concert begins.

like this: The groom and bride bought a half liter of *palinka* [Hungarian liqueur] and invited the other Rom to come over and celebrate. Actually they didn't have to formally invite anyone. The Rom knew whenever a wedding was taking place and came on their own accord. Then they started to drink. The *palinka* went around and around until there was nothing left. With the bottle finished one of the guests would throw his coat on the floor, followed by whatever amount of money he had in his pocket, thirty-five or seventy-five cents. All his money was thrown onto the coat. Then others began to throw money onto the coat. With this money they bought food and drink. The women went home to prepare the meal while the men sang, danced, and played music. The food was brought back, a sheet was spread on the floor, and the food was laid out on the sheet. There were no chairs or tables. The celebrating continued through the night and only cost the bride and groom half a liter of *palinka*.

We used to stay away from the Hungarians as children and they did the same as well. We were afraid they would beat us up and they were afraid we would steal from them. As children we wouldn't dare go to the market or to the movies. But now, thank God, it's different. Now the Rom man marries a Hungarian woman. There are many mixed marriages here in Hodász. It is not a problem these days as it used to be. In many ways we are more decent than they are because the Rom do not drink or fight, and aren't sexually promiscuous as the Hungarians are. You can ask the mayor, he will tell you the same thing.

RIGHT
Hodász, Hungary: Rom children joining their voices in an impromptu concert

Hodász, Hungary *Zoltan Howáth* (age 15)

I was born in Hodász, which is to say I was born in a boring town. Sometimes with my friends we travel to Nagykálló or even Nyíregyháza, where there are more things to do. We travel by horse and wagon. It is a lot cheaper to feed the horse some hay and oats than it is to buy gasoline. Everything has become so expensive since our government became democratic that I hear people talk about how it was better under the Communists. Personally I disagree. The Communists were some of the biggest thieves. The police protected them as if they were a private militia for the Communists. The police definitely are not the friends of the Rom. I am worried because the Rom in Romania are being attacked by the *gaje* and this prejudice has come here. Many *gaje* are speaking out, saying we are lazy, stealing, and doing nothing productive for the country. My father works repairing bathtubs, water heaters, stoves, and other things like that. Most of his work comes from the *gaje*. Is he unproductive? What *gajo* is doing this kind of work here in Hodász?

I have thought about becoming an actor when I'm older. Pretending you are somebody else and making the audience believe you is a wonderful power to have. It is in our blood to be entertainers. The best musicians and dancers in Hungary are the Rom. This is a tradition we brought with us as we wandered through Europe from India. It won't be easy to study acting because I will have to move to Budapest. Going to school and living in Budapest will be very expensive.

Hodász, Hungary: Zoltan Howáth (right) and his friend Jolán

Utu Šavo
(My Boy)

Hungarian Romungro Rom
Allegro moderato

Arranged and transcribed by
Yale Strom

Ut-u ša-vo so tu ker - ta _____ Řomnia čha-te pa-ša-man-

te _____ Ro - ma le Ša - va -le Ke - re man___ ge _____ bu - ja - re

8va 2nd & 3rd time

pa - ša-man-te me tej a - bej _____ Ro - ma-le Ša-va-le

1.,2.   3.   Fine

Ke - re man - ge___ bu-ja-re pa - ša mante me tej a - bej _____ bej _____

My boy, what have you done?
Romni woman, what did I do?
Rom brothers,
I want her to come back to me.

Rom brothers,
I want her to come back home,
back home to me.

(The English translation does not correspond line by line with each verse.)

Vilok, Ukraine: A Rom house

UKRAINE

There are no official historical writings that tell of the Rom being in Russia before 1500, but it is believed they inhabited the Carpathian region of southeastern Ukraine probably sixty to eighty years earlier. This assumption is based upon the fact that the Rom were in Transylvania (then under Hungarian rule) by 1417. Some of these Rom were slaves who had escaped from the Turkish vassal states of Moldavia and Wallachia. After they escaped, some traveled the spine of the Carpathian Mountains, which reaches into the Maramureş area (northwestern Romania), north across the Tisza River, into Carpathian-Ukraine, where they settled.

During my field research in this region of the Ukraine, I met some Rom who said they still traveled through the Carpathians into the Maramureş region for trade purposes. They said they followed the same route their ancestors had taken nearly five hundred years before.

Little has been written about the Rom specifically in Ukraine. Before the Ukraine regained its independence in 1991, it had been a land under the rule of many other countries: Poland, czarist Russia, the Austro-Hungarian Empire (only the Carpathian and Bukovina regions), Czechoslovakia, Hungary, and the Soviet Union. Thus the history of the Rom in the Carpathian-Ukraine is similar to that of their brethren in those countries today.

During the early years of the former Soviet Union (1917–1991), the government treated the Rom as equal citizens and as a distinct minority with full rights of self-expression. The Rom had their own newspaper printed in Romani, and in 1925 Teater Romen (the Rom Theater) was established in Moscow. After Lenin died and Stalin came to power, the Rom, like many other minorities (particularly the Jews), were forced to abandon much of their culture and traditions. During the harsh Stalinist years, the government abolished the Rom's nomadic life-style, demanded assimilation, and forced many to live and work on collective farms in the republics of Russia, Ukraine, Moldavia, and Belorussia (Belarus).

During World War II, many Rom fought bravely in various Soviet military units. Because of their keen knowledge of horses they were especially helpful in the vital final offensive, which drove the

Germans out of Soviet territory in the fall of 1944. During the bitter cold winter of 1943–1944, many of the Soviet supply lines to their men on the Russian front were kept open by their cavalry on horseback, which included some Rom. The snowy and icy terrain made it too difficult to travel with the motorized military vehicles.

After the war the discrimination against the Rom began again with renewed intensity. Similar to the discrimination suffered by the Jews, the Rom were forced to stop speaking Romani in public and were compelled to live double lives. Outside of their homes and at work they were supposed to be dutiful Soviets, while in their homes they stealthily preserved their culture as best as they could.

There were some Rom who did prosper during the Communist years as the Soviet people always held a high regard for their bohemian music and dance. A few Rom became famous and traveled the world, working in the Soviet circuses, Rom Theater, and music ensembles. Others completed school and studied at the university, which enabled them to become teachers, engineers, et cetera. But the one right the Rom longed for the most—along with virtu-ally all of Soviet society—was the privilege of being able to travel and visit family and friends in Europe. Not being able to travel officially was the cruelest law against the Rom. Not allowing a Rom to travel, one of his main defining characteristics, was similar to imprisonment. Consequently, the lifting of travel sanctions for all the people in the new independent Ukraine was a great source of relief.

Though the Rom have the right to travel outside the Ukraine today, it is still quite difficult for them to cross into the republics of Slovakia, Hungary, or Romania. These governments are not eager to allow easy access for the Rom because they view them as a social people with nothing substantial to offer. As these countries' economies worsen, they want to contain their own native Rom populations and, if anything, have their numbers decrease by encouraging emigration.

Today in the entire Ukraine there are about 350,000 Rom. Most of the Rom speak Hungarian as their first language and, like their fellow ethnic Hungarians in Vinogradov and throughout Carpathian-Ukraine, their patriotic allegiance, deep in their hearts, is with Hungary.

Vinogradov, Ukraine: The former Jewish quarter

Vinogradov, Ukraine *Valentin Kallov Valentinovič* (age 32)

Vinogradov, Ukraine: Valentin Kallov Valentinovič

The Čop train station was humming with people buying and selling all kinds of wares and foreign currencies. Because Čop is on the border of Ukraine and Hungary, people from the republics of the former Soviet Union come to the station to meet and do business with travelers. After a while in this smoke-filled environment I decided to get some fresh air and buy some ice cream, the only food edible at the station. Here I met Julia, a woman in her late fifties, who was waiting for her granddaughter to arrive after four days on the train from Siberia. Julia had overheard me tell another lady that I was traveling to Vinogradov. Julia came over to me, introduced herself, and said if I had no specific place to stay in Vinogradov, I could stay with her. I gladly accepted her invitation.

I began playing the violin at the age of six. My teacher was Anton Gergelyi. I learned with him in the music school. He was a great teacher and even better man. At the school I learned to play classical music, but I've been playing Rom music since I can remember with my father being my teacher. I passed the entrance exam for the music high school but for financial reasons I couldn't continue. I had to help my mother since my father had left us, so I began playing in the local restaurants. My mother works now selling flowers and vegetables at the open market in the main square, but some days it is very difficult for her to go out because she has bad asthma. We don't have the money to buy the proper medicine for her and even if we did have the money you can't find that special inhaler anywhere here. Up until about two years ago I was playing regularly at the restaurants here in Nagyszöllös [Hungarian for Vinogradov] and in other places in the Carpathians. It was lucrative but now there are too many musicians, not enough work available, and a poor economy. I have been forced to work in a factory with heavy machinery to help support my mother, wife, and son. The work is hard and dangerous for my hands. I regret having to do it. My fingers hurt me and make it difficult to play the violin. What can I do?

We are good musicians because music is an inborn trait among most Rom. When a good musician has a son, the son begins learning to play, dance, and sing as soon as he is able to walk, even sometimes before learning to speak. The son constantly watches his father practice and when he is five or six years old the father takes him to some of his music jobs. Rom music is a vital part of our heritage

Vilok, Ukraine: An impromptu concert of Rom, Jewish, and jazz music, with Valentin (left) playing obbligato violin

and can only be learned in this way. It is impossible, impossible to really understand, feel, and properly perform the music if one learned it only in school.

As you can see, I'm not wearing anything fancy right now. I have a few nice clothes but not many because of the expense. But for me my regal clothing is my music. When I play, I feel as if I am wrapped up in the most luxurious suit fit for a king. Without music I would be naked and alone. This is why I am teaching my son, Sáni, to play the violin so he, too, can pass on this vital tradition of ours to his son. Because of our wanderings we have learned to be masters of imitation, copying the *gajo*'s religion, language, food, dress, and even music. In fact we can play their music often much better than they can play it themselves. But can they play or sing our music half as well as us? Rarely. I realize this might sound a bit boastful but would you rather have a Rom playing a Hungarian rhapsody or a *gajo*?

The train ride to Vinogradov was a memorable one. It was early evening and the beauty of the sunset casting itself over the rolling green Carpathian Mountains was magnificent. The train itself was old, with rows of wooden benches, open seating, and wood-framed windows. Everything and everybody was crowded together, occupying all the seats and floor space. There were Rom, Ruthenians, Ukrainians, Russians, Hungarians, and one American. There were railroad workers, farmers, teachers, construction workers, clerks, and students, carrying suitcases and wicker baskets full of fruits, vegetables, dried meats, stereos, radios, clothes, new bicycles, geese, ducks, cats, and even children.

I sat next to two young Rom men who were quite curious about my cameras and my reason for traveling to Vinogradov. They were surprised and laughed loudly when I told them I was writing a book about the Rom. After some picture taking and the exchanging of addresses they invited me to visit them in Vilok, a small village near Vinogradov.

When we arrived, it was dark. Most everyone either walked or rode a bicycle home. The town had no taxis or buses, few private cars and trucks, and even fewer streetlamps. At nighttime everyone walked in the middle of the dirt streets. As we walked home, I explained to Julia in Yiddish, a little Polish, and even less Hungarian what brought me to her town.

FAR LEFT
Vilok, Ukraine: Julia Kobrin taking the train home to Vinogradov, after a long day in Čop
LEFT
Vilok, Ukraine: A Rom lumberjack coming home from work

Julia lived in a home she and her husband, János, had built themselves. There was no hot water and only an outhouse for a toilet in the backyard. When you walked to the outhouse, you passed a vegetable garden, a lush vineyard, chickens, roosters, and pigs. János and Julia were retired farmers who had brought some of the farm to the city while maintaining a bigger farm out in the country. After a hearty and delicious dinner of fresh eggs and milk, green onions, tomatoes, carrots, and strawberries from their garden I was shown to my room. In a comfortable bed I fell fast asleep, having hardly slept at all in the last week.

In Vinogradov the following morning I met Anton Gergelyi, a retired music teacher who had taught in the town's only high school. With his help I met several of his former Rom students, all of whom spoke highly and kindly of Anton.

The Rom for the most part did not live in Vinogradov or in the other larger cities in Carpathian-Ukraine, but in the smaller villages like Vilok. One of Anton's former star pupils was Valentin. Valentin agreed to go with me to Vilok, where his younger brother lived. When I met Valentin at the train station, I had my violin and he had his, except he had no case, he just held it casually under his arm. While waiting for the train, he and I played Jewish and Rom music, entertaining the other passengers on the platform.

Vinogradov, Ukraine *Lajos Lelki* (age 57)

I began learning the cymbalom when I was seven years old from my father. When I was seventeen, I quit playing the cymbalom and apprenticed as a painter. I had to earn money for our home because both my parents were sick. It was impossible to make a living as a musician. When I finished my apprenticeship, I became a church painter. Once while painting a church, I fell from the ladder and broke my arm quite severely. The doctor told my mother that the bones in my wrist had broken in such a way that I would probably lose most of my movement and certainly not play any instrument again. My mother paid the doctor for setting the bones but then took me to this Rom woman we called *phuri bibi* [old aunt]. She was known in the Rom community as one who had special healing powers. She put some kind of putrid salve on my

ABOVE
Vinogradov, Ukraine: Valentin playing first violin and Lajos playing second violin (harmony) in the Valentinovičs' backyard
RIGHT
Vinogradov, Ukraine: Lajos Lelki relaxing in his backyard

wrist. It smelled so bad, it made me choke and my eyes water. She had of course taken off the splint the doctor had put on. Every day for the next six weeks my mother put on that salve and then massaged and exercised my wrist and arm. To this day I still don't know what that special salve was, but my wrist healed completely without any effects of arthritis. I still do some painting and playing the second violin in restaurants. But money is scarce these days and musicians are some of the last people to receive it.

In Nagyszöllös we aren't bothered by the *gaje*, probably due to the fact we aren't very many here. However, sometimes when I'm walking down the street, I can feel the stares and see a slight change in behavior of a shopkeeper when I enter his store. I don't take offense to it. It's a kind of learned habit, out of ignorance. Most everyone knows me in town since I painted many of the buildings and homes here. On one hand I enjoy the familiarity, on the other hand I am Rom and I have wanderlust in my veins. If I was young again, I would love to travel the world and see such exotic countries as Tibet, China, Egypt, and Brazil. The excitement of travel is not knowing who you will meet along the way in a hotel, café, tavern, or on the road. The *gaje* say, read a book and go traveling. We say, go traveling and read a different book every time you meet a person in a new destination. I guess there is a little Rom blood in you.

TOP LEFT
Vilok, Ukraine: The transport of hay is a daily chore.
BOTTOM LEFT
Vilok, Ukraine: Signs pointing out the directions to the nearest large cities. The signs are written in Ukrainian Cyrillic and Hungarian, the two main languages in the Carpathian-Ukraine region.
RIGHT
Vinogradov, Ukraine: Mrs. Valentinovič with freshly picked parsley from her garden

Vilok, Ukraine: Kati Palotás on the bridge that spans the Tisza River

Vilok, Ukraine *Kati Palotás* (age 13)

Vilok is a small town but I like it. All of the Rom live in one part of the town. We feel more secure and comfortable being around our own kind. I'll probably always live here even when I become a mother, but I would like to travel to America someday. I'd like to visit Chicago, where all the gangsters live, and be able to buy some fancy clothes. Of course I only know America from the movies and television programs I have seen. I remember seeing one American movie, I can't remember the name of it, but Sylvester Stallone was in it. There was a scene where a guy is waiting for a taxi, one stops and the driver rolls down his window, but the man at the curb tells him he is waiting for a Gypsy cabdriver. When this specific car and driver drive by, the man gets in and they speed off. This Gypsy driver was a black man. What did they mean by Gypsy taxi driver?

Generally I do things with my Rom friends, though sometime we visit and play with the *gaje*. There isn't a lot to do here in this town. We have one movie theater and a place where we can play billiards. Most of the time we go for walks, fish out of the Tisza River, dance, swim, listen to music, or go over to someone's house to watch TV. Though my family is poor, I'm not envious of what others have. When you are envious of somebody else, you only see the good things he has, never the bad stuff. He may have an illness or parents who are mean, one never knows. I only wish my father had a better job and could earn more money. He works at the shoe factory and they pay poorly. The *gajo* thinks the Rom's life is always full of happiness, song, and dance. They don't know the stress my father has trying to provide for a family of eight.

Vilok, Ukraine: Rom girls strolling on the bridge that connects Ukraine to Hungary, crossing the Tisza River

Vilok, Ukraine: Alexander Sándor Virág playing his accordion in his home

Vilok, Ukraine *Alexander Sándor Virág* (age 33)

I was born in Vilok in a poor family. There wasn't enough money for me to study, so instead of being a burden at home I left for two years at the age of fifteen, playing music to survive. During those two years, I got married and traveled all over Europe, playing in restaurants from Ungvár [Uzhgorod] to Frankfurt. I taught myself how to play the accordion beginning at the age of ten. Music was of course the mainstay of our family. My father, Lajos Duni, was a great violinist, the best in the Carpathians. He also traveled the world using music as his ticket. Now I play in the Ukrainian Philharmonic Symphony Orchestra, when they need an accordionist. I also work evenings locally and outside of the town in restaurants, playing music.

These days the economic situation here has been horrific. If someone has a regular job, he or she must also work by selling anything on the black market to earn some extra money. Life has become harder for us since Ukraine declared its independence. We get some child support from the state but everything is so expensive we spend more than we receive. It is not easy to support a wife and four children. The schools have become worse, too, with our children learning very little. They haven't motivated them, so it seems they don't want to learn anything, even a musical instrument. All the children want to do is play in the streets, listen and dance to music, and go to the movie theater.

Vilok, Ukraine *Brigita Móskus* (age 16)

Vilok, Ukraine: Brigita Móskus and her friends

In school I'm not learning anything. I have many friends who finished school in the eighth grade and cannot even sign their name. Often the teachers are just chatting, drinking coffee, and wandering about the school as if they were on one long lunch break. But despite the miserably boring environment at school I am learning a little there, but more at home. My mother doesn't read or write but she has repeatedly stressed the importance of reading and writing so I do my best to learn at home. I want to be a writer and write true stories about the Rom of the Carpathians. Most of what the *gaje* know about us is written by them for them, and is negative. Just our folktales alone I think would be fascinating for the *gaje* to read and learn something about our old and rich culture.

Vilok, Ukraine: Enjoying a cold drink on a hot day at a rest stop on the Hungarian-Ukrainian border

On the outskirts of Vilok was the Rom quarter with one narrow dirt road running through the middle of it. If I hadn't known any better, it could have been a scene from the village in Poland where my grandparents grew up just before World War I. The wooden houses with shingled roofs were small, with an open porch in the front. In front of the homes were vegetable gardens, sleeping dogs, clothes hung out to dry, and women sitting on stoops preparing food. With the front doors open, chickens and geese freely sauntered in and out.

Vilok, Ukraine: Rom children and adults on the only street that goes through the Rom neighborhood

Vilok, Ukraine: There is no indoor plumbing in the Rom quarters of Vilok, so washing oneself and one's clothes must be done in a washbasin.

Vilok, Ukraine: Rom children playing in the street

At the end of the long, hot day I had made friends with many of the Rom children in the neighborhood. Wherever I walked with my cameras and violin in hand, they followed closely behind, incessantly asking me to take their photograph and to play the violin.

Song of Ulök

Transcribed and arranged by Yale Strom

Vinogradov, Ukraine: Zoltan accompanying his nephew Sáni on the guitar while Sáni's mother listens

Stockholm, Sweden: Downtown Stockholm is built on an archipelago.

SWEDEN

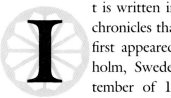It is written in the town chronicles that the Rom first appeared in Stockholm, Sweden, in September of 1511. They arrived on St. Michael's Day and told the public they were from Little Egypt. The Swedes noticed their dark hair and swarthy complexions and heard a strange language being spoken. Consequently, they thought these Rom were from the Tartar tribe, and thus they were called *Tattare*. These Rom had trekked from Russia through the Karelia region bordering Russia and Finland, then through Lapland and into Sweden. Initially, the *gaje* welcomed the Rom but soon afterward developed animosity toward them. The Rom wandered in the rural areas of southern Sweden because the weather was not quite as harsh as it was in the northern provinces. The peasants accused them of pilfering from their fields and farms and leaving large amounts of refuse behind in their encampments.

In 1637, the Swedish government, inspired by laws in Denmark and Norway, expelled the Rom from the entire country.

In the late nineteenth century through the eve of World War I, restrictions barring Rom from Sweden were eased. Kalderash Rom from Russia, who were coppersmiths and artisans, and Lowara Rom from Hungary (via France), who were horse handlers, migrated to Sweden.

During this period the most well-known Rom family in Sweden today established roots in the country. In 1900 Konri Taikon, who was born in Hungary, traveled from Russia and settled with his wife, Voroshana, in Haparanda, Sweden. They had eleven children, most of whom became artists or musicians. Two of the most famous Taikons were Katarina, a writer, and Rosa, a silversmith. Both women were known to many *gaje* in Sweden. For a Rom to marry into the Taikon family was, and still is, a great honor.

With the start of World War I, in 1914, the Swedish government decided to take an aggressive position of political isolationism. Sweden was officially neutral during the war and stopped most immigration until 1954. For certain "undesirable" races and ethnicities it was next to impossible to enter Swe-

Rinkeby, Sweden: The fruit-and-vegetable market

den. Officially, only four Rom entered Sweden illegally during this forty-year period. Two Rom from Norway and two from Poland managed to sneak across the border and escape the Nazi terror.

In 1914 there were some two hundred Rom in Sweden. Between the two world wars the men worked in their traditional jobs: copperware repair, scrap-metal collecting and selling, horse breaking, music, dance, and carnival work, while the women told fortunes.

In the 1940s the Rom were confronted with economic misfortune: The copperware repair business was disappearing due to the advent of rust-free steel and aluminum products. And the

Rom dance bands and other traveling entertainers were forced to travel to remote villages because of the strong competition from the *gaje* musicians in the towns and cities. The situation forced many Rom to leave their traditional occupations and seek work as junk-car dealers, miners, and laborers in heavy industries. Some steps were taken by the government to alleviate the Rom's hardships in these years. The most significant step was establishing schools for the children in tents at the sites of their encampments. The government paid *gaje* teachers to travel with the Rom throughout the country. The first such school opened in 1933 in Sundsvall. Still, in 1943, only 15 percent of the

Swedish Rom could read and write.

After World War II several Rom refugees were brought from the concentration camps to Sweden for rehabilitation. One of these Rom Holocaust survivors was Sofia Breginska, who was born in Poland in 1931. Her family was nomadic. When the Germans and Russians completely occupied Poland on September 27, 1939, Sofia, her family, and other Rom from the village were taken by the Gestapo to a labor camp. In February 1940, she and her family were transferred to Auschwitz. Upon arrival she was painfully tattooed with an electric pen on her left arm with the identification number *Z 4515*. The Rom sent to the various death camps in Central and Eastern Europe had a *Z* for *Zigeuner* (German for Rom) and the numbers for registration tattooed on their arms.

When she arrived in the camp she was nine years old. For five years and three months Sofia lived with constant pain, hunger, fatigue, and fear of death. Her youth vanished in Auschwitz.

The camp was surrounded by barbed wire charged with high-voltage electricity. In the watchtowers stood soldiers with their machine guns trained on the prisoners. Sofia worked breaking up stones and carting away dirt. In the beginning she sometimes happened to see her parents, sisters, and brothers. After some time her family disappeared one by one in the gas chambers.

At the end of the war the Russian soldiers liberated Sofia and other prisoners in Auschwitz. She was among those taken to Sweden by the Swedish Red Cross.

When Sofia was brought to Sweden she could not read or write but she could speak her Romani dialect, Polish, Russian, Czech, and German, and she understood Yiddish. She quickly learned to speak Swedish and eventually married into the Taikon family.

In the mid-1960s the Swedish government began building public housing for the Rom and other immigrants in Stockholm and Göteborg and giving them social and monetary assistance. The word about Sweden's benevolence for émigrés (particularly political refugees) quickly spread throughout Europe and the Middle East, encouraging waves of immigration. In the 1970s Rom from Western Europe began migrating to Sweden. Then, in the 1980s, with the upheaval and opening of the borders in the former Eastern Bloc countries, Rom from these countries began arriving as well.

Nearly 80 percent of the approximately 7,500 to 8,000 Rom in Sweden today arrived after 1954. Recently, however, nationalism and the clamor for jobs for natives have caused a rise in racism. Sweden is no longer a guaranteed haven for the Rom.

After arriving in Stockholm, Sweden, I wasted little time in beginning my work. My second day there I took the subway to the historical district of the city known as Old Town. There I met a filmmaker who was making a film about a Rom boy who was a boxer. He was going to be busy for several days before he could introduce me to this boy and other Rom so I decided to go out on my own. After lunch I took the subway to Rinkeby, a suburb outside of Stockholm.

Rinkeby, Sweden: Johnny Columbus in his school library

Rinkeby, Sweden *Johnny Columbus* (age 16)

My father was born in Spain and my mother here in Sweden. Every year we travel to Spain and France. We live in our summer home in Barcelona. Most of our friends there and here are Rom. I was born a Rom and one must accept how he was born. If not life will be long and unforgiving.

Rom are all like brothers. For example, if my mother gave me money for milk and bread at 8 A.M. and I lived in a Rom town, I would visit with all my friends along the way to the store, maybe drinking some tea and eating some food in various homes. I wouldn't return to my mother's until late afternoon. We enjoy the real essence of life—life itself, the events that transpire in the course of a normal day. This is why we don't steer our own country. Perhaps we don't have the discipline to govern ourselves like the *gajo* has.

Here in Rinkeby we are mostly people of color—Turks, Africans, Kurds—so there is little racism here. But in the center of Stockholm when I walk around I can feel the eyes of the Swedes who stare at me with distrust. If I speak with a Swede who doesn't know me and I tell him I live in Rinkeby, immediately he thinks of certain things. We are poor, dirty, lazy, steal, and do drugs. Well, I have seen poor, dirty, and lazy Swedes in Old Town who are high on drugs. Does this mean everyone in Old Town is like this?

Rom culture seems to be not so strong here in Sweden as it is in the warmer countries like Italy, France, and Spain. In the warmer lands you can live outside in caravans. When we travel to our relatives in Spain, we live in our trailer, often sleeping outside at night. In Sweden we travel around the country together with maybe ten other families, living in campgrounds. But in the autumn and winter it's too cold to live in caravans. If I move when I become older, it will probably be to Spain. There the *gaje* take more time to talk with you while you walk the streets and you are often invited to share a coffee or tea with a complete stranger. In Sweden they have to have a holiday or a birthday to have a reason to invite you to their home.

You know, I think one of the reasons the *gaje* dislike the Rom is because they are jealous of us. They think we are lazy and only live off of the social welfare the gov-

Rinkeby is where many immigrants have settled. There are Turks, Arabs, Kurds, Africans, South Americans, Greeks, Serbians, Finns, and Rom. Many of the immigrants left their homelands because they were being persecuted by their governments for their political beliefs. Others came seeking a better living. Many of the people in Rinkeby were unemployed, poor, and received some welfare from the Swedish government. When I mentioned to several Swedes that I was doing some work in Rinkeby, often a kind of quizzical look appeared on their faces. Rinkeby was considered an area that was dangerous, with a higher rate of crime than any other area of Stockholm. For me, traveling to Rinkeby meant entering a fascinating and hospitable Rom world.

While I was walking in the main shopping square in Rinkeby, some young Turkish boys came up to me and started asking all sorts of questions about America. Afterward I asked them if there were some Rom around here. "Everywhere," they yelled, and they proceeded to call two teenage boys over to us. Both boys, Antonio Atanasio and Johnny Columbus, were walking home from school.

Antonio invited me to his home, where he lived with his grandparents Sonya and Bua. Their home was extremely neat and clean, with typical Rom decor. On the floors were Middle Eastern carpets, the windows were framed with beautiful curtains, and religious paintings hung on the walls. The rooms were not cluttered with an unnecessary amount of furniture and trinkets and there were very few books.

Before I began to do some interviewing, Antonio, his cousin Alex, and his uncle Stevo took me to a bedroom, where they played the guitar and sang some superb Rom songs. Then it was my turn. Out came my violin and I began to play some Jewish and Rom music for them. This immediately attracted everyone in the home to the bedroom. There were twelve of us now crowded into this small bedroom. After an hour of music and song Sonya invited me to the kitchen for some tea and sandwiches.

ernment gives us every month. I can't say some of us don't receive some help, but $375 a month isn't enough to live on here in Sweden. A normal salary for a working-class *gajo* is about $1,600 to $2,000 a month. Rom aren't the only people here in Rinkeby that receive some social welfare. The Turks, Kurds, and Ethiopians get money, too. Our fathers find it difficult to be employed by the *gaje*, who would rather give the job to a Swede. Therefore most Rom men work for themselves. My father works hard traveling throughout Stockholm sharpening all kinds of knives and tools. At a normal job you know exactly what you will receive at the end of the month and the complete amount will be there, 100 percent. But when you are working as we do, you never know exactly from month to month how much you'll earn. Some months a great deal, other times very little. All the *gaje* do is complain about us without really knowing who we are.

Rinkeby, Sweden   *Sonya Atanasio* (age 65)

I was born in Budapest. My father was Italian and my mother Hungarian. Before the war my two brothers, sister, parents, and myself traveled by car through Italy, Morocco, Spain, France, Germany, and Belgium. My father was a coppersmith and we traveled with him as he searched for work. He had a very good business. We would work during the day and then eat, drink, dance, sing, and play music by a large fire at night. Music is in our blood and our passion for music is passed on from one generation to the next. When we finally would go to sleep, we slept in beautiful, colorful tents. I loved the life. When the war began, we were taken as prisoners to a labor camp in northern Italy. There we stayed under

Rinkeby, Sweden: Sonya Atanasio on her balcony

harsh conditions for four years until the Americans liberated the camp. My grandparents weren't as lucky as us. They were taken along with thousands of other Rom from eastern Hungary to Poland, where they were killed in Auschwitz. After the war my father began selling and fixing things for the many refugees. Again he had a good business. We traveled throughout Europe until the late sixties. My sister at that time had moved to Sweden. When my father died, we all decided to come to live in Sweden because we knew the government helped the Rom with money and housing. Life has been easier here but I miss those times when we were traveling, especially in Italy and in France. The music, the songs, the sky above us. In Sweden much of our culture is vanishing and this saddens me. When the children grow up, they don't stay near their parents like they used to.

The kitchen in most Rom homes I visited throughout Europe was the focal room of the house. Here eating, entertaining, and discussions of all kinds took place. In addition to this, there was the constant whistling of the teakettle or, in some homes, the samovar.

It was in Sonya's kitchen that I met her husband, Bua—the much respected patriarch of the family and community. There were often as many as eighteen family members visiting Sonya's home at the same time.

Rinkeby, Sweden *Alexander "Burca" Kwiek* (age 13)

Rinkeby, Sweden: Alexander Kwiek taking a break during his practice session at the boxing club

Rinkeby, Sweden: Alexander Kwiek's training partner Fardi Bessik

They opened the boxing club last year. That's when I began to box. I plan to continue my whole life. It's fun. Maybe I'll be a champion and a big star. Whatever one wants, one can become. I have had nine matches and I won eight of them. I'm third in my weight class in all of Sweden. I took the bronze medal in a match in Göteborg. My friend Fardi, he is the champion in his weight class in Sweden and second in all of Scandinavia. Even though Mike Tyson is in prison now, I still think he is the best in the world. But I also like George Foreman because he has proven to the world that becoming older is no reason one should not have dreams. My favorite boxer of all times is Rocky Marciano.

My parents were born in Poland, and I was born in Västerås, Sweden. My father sells carpets while my mother cleans the house, washes the dishes, cooks the food, and takes care of my sister, who is three years old. My parents read and write Romani. I can't but they will teach me. Last year my grandpa died in his bed. We ate a big meal prepared with the kind of food that he enjoyed. We didn't play any music and we had to wear something black to remember him—not to mourn him—for one year. Grandpa Buzui was a good man. I miss him.

Rinkeby, Sweden   *Cherry Kwiek* (age 16)

I was born in Sweden and my parents were born in Poland. I've been to Poland once but I didn't exactly like it there. All my relatives have moved to either Sweden or Germany. I quit school last year. My parents didn't want me to finish. But if I had put pressure on my mother, she would have probably let me go to college. My cousin is in college studying to be a doctor. It is customary for Rom girls who are fourteen or fifteen years old to leave school, because most are getting married at that age. My mother was fourteen when she was married. I don't know if I'm getting married soon or not. You see, it goes like this: Another family will come over to our house and speak to my parents about their son marrying me. If my parents want to, they discuss it with me. And if I say no, it's no. But if I say yes, we could be married in a year, or a month, even in a week. As a wife my job is to stay home, cook, clean, take care of the children, and teach them about the Rom culture. It is possible for a Rom boy or girl to marry a *gajo* but it's really not okay. Rom would rather keep to themselves.

Some Rom kids have problems with alcohol and drugs. Maybe they have problems at home. Some take drugs or drink because of the peer pressure. Luckily my mind is too strong for this and I never paid any attention to their talk and name-calling, from the Swedes or Rom.

I'm not sure what it means to be a Rom. I know I am a human like any other person. I'm proud I was born a Rom and always will tell people I am Rom.

Rinkeby, Sweden: Cherry Kwiek

During my travels most of the Rom I met became much more receptive to me when they were told I was Jewish. They felt a kinship with me and with the Jewish people for several reasons. The first and foremost reason was the Rom had suffered the tragedy of the Holocaust along with the Jews. The Rom and the Jews were the only ethnic groups singled out by Hitler for complete annihilation. The Rom had wandered throughout Europe, often being expelled from one country to another. This happened to the Jews as well. When there was a problem in a community, or something terrible happened, who was quick to be blamed, harassed, and punished? The Rom or the Jews. Finally the Rom admired the Jews' perseverance and ultimate success over the oppression of the *gaje*. The kindred feeling the Rom had for the Jews was clear to me when I was told by a Rom, "Yale, we don't consider you like the other *gaje*."

Rinkeby, Sweden: Mrs. Koka, a Rom originally from France

Rinkeby, Sweden *Lula Sabas* (age 29)

I can read and write but my parents and husband cannot, so I'm helping them often. It was common for my parents' generation to have so few Rom who could read and write, but they all spoke several languages. I speak Romani, English, Spanish, and Swedish. My children are going to school so they can learn to read and write. I want them to be able to get a good job like becoming a coppersmith. If one is able to work with his hands, he can travel and find work anywhere in the world. It is better to have a job than live from the social welfare. Most Rom receive some money from the Swedish government. You get used to expecting this help and it takes your incentive away to provide for yourself. And when they give you this money, they make many decisions for you. Where shall you live? What you must teach your children and so on.

Some of the negative things a *gajo* may think of when he hears the word *Gypsy* sometimes are true. First let me say clearly that in the past many minorities had to resort to actions that are not acceptable to the majority. Sometimes you will do anything to get some money for some food for your children and yourself. It is true that some Rom in the past, and still today, kidnap children and sell them to the *gaje*. Recently in Germany two children were kidnapped and sold to Rom women here in Sweden. They couldn't have children and the authorities wouldn't let them adopt. In France many Rom families from Yugoslavia sell their children because they have too many and are too poor to care for and feed them all. They sell them cheap to *gaje* who want to adopt but don't want to bother with all the legal matters and paperwork.

Rom culture has changed here in the last twenty years.

Rinkeby, Sweden: Lula Sabas and her two children in their home

Now you see some married women who don't put any-thing like a scarf in their hair. I don't like that. And more women are doing some kind of work outside of their homes. When my youngest, who is four years old, will start school maybe I'll go back to being a secretary. My husband doesn't mind. Our clothing has changed but we haven't forgotten our language or where we came from. We are from India and somehow we split up. That is why we are all over the world. But the history that is most important for us today is that of World War II. I know Rom who had family who were killed by the Nazis. It didn't matter if you came from a family where the father was a *gajo* and the mother was Rom, the Germans still killed you. Being Rom comes from the father. If your father marries a *gajo,* you are still Rom.

Rinkeby, Sweden: Another member of the Kwiek family and his Nigerian friend

Rinkeby, Sweden: Antonio Atanasio, holding photographs of his grandmother, Sonya, during her younger years

Rinkeby, Sweden *Antonio Atanasio* (age 16)

I was born in Paris and after a short stay in Belgium came to Sweden at the age of six. My parents are divorced so I live with my grandparents Sonya and Bua. Among my Rom friends I speak only Romani. In our home my grandmother tries to keep most of the Rom traditions. She cooks *sarmi,* which is a Rom dish. You take hamburger, rice, and paprika, mix it all together, and stuff it into cabbage leaves. It's delicious.

At school I'm in a class that only has Rom in it. Our teacher is cool and allows us to learn not only about Swedish culture but also about Rom culture, too. I'm not that interested in school, though I know it's important. Learning to read and write is a necessity if you want to succeed like my father. But I'd rather be outside breathing the fresh air and messing around. There are many old Rom who can't read or write and this can be a problem if they have no one around to help them. If they buy a VCR and they don't know how to install it, they have to read the instructions, but if they can't read, they become a prisoner within their own mind.

I'll get married probably in two or three years. We will have children but how many children only God knows. But I do know I will be successful like my father. Selling cars, carpets, anything which can be bought I will sell except drugs.

Rinkeby, Sweden: Many Rom youth attend special classes that cater to their specific cultural needs

Lund, Sweden   *Pukla Lakatos* (age 38)

People say that the times are changing. I agree one has to be open to modern influences. I understand our young are changing, but certain Rom traditions will never be changed. Here in Sweden a young boy or girl eighteen, nineteen years old will leave their home, let us say from Malmö, and move to Kiruna in Norrlands. Maybe they don't visit their parents for a year, or two years, or even six or seven. We Rom don't do this. Am I so tired that I can't visit my parents? Is my relationship with them finished when I become married and move out of the home? We try to live near our parents, and if we don't, then we make sure to visit them as often as possible.

Prejudice and belief in God are in complete opposition to each other. I am a preacher and have read the Bible many times, dissecting each sentence for its true meaning. We have accepted God and his teachings. We are the same in front of God's eyes as are the Jews, Greeks, and Arabs. If I cut my leg, it bleeds the same color as the Swede who cuts his leg. Then why do people lighter than I travel to Spain to become brown like me? Are they so dumb that they will pay thousands of dollars to have brown skin like me only to return and say I'm too dark? Is there a difference between one's skin which is burned brown by the sun and my skin color which comes from my family's genes?

Our history hasn't been written down. We have the tradition of passing it down from one generation to another through the telling of long epic stories called *parameetchi* in Romani.

Lund, Sweden: Pukla Lakatos

These stories and many others like it are our memorials. We lost over half a million people in the war, but we don't have any large monuments or institutions in the world like the Jews have that remind and teach the world about our tragedy. Look how quickly the world has forgotten, with the recent deportations by the German government of the Rom back to Romania, where many of them are being persecuted. A Rom may forget about God during his daily life, but Hitler's atrocities he will never forget.

Rinkeby, Sweden *Bruno "Bua" Kwiek* (age 38)

Rinkeby, Sweden: Bruno "Bua" Kwiek sitting in Sonya's kitchen

Many of our customs are very old, passed down from one generation to the next. When a young man and girl are to get married, usually their parents have introduced them to each other. The boy can say no and so can the girl but usually the parents have spoken to them about each other and they of course have met in person. The groom then must pay something to the bride's father. The amount depends on how beautiful she is [laughter]. . . . Actually the amount depends on what sort of family the boy comes from. Does he, or will he, have a good job and so on. When this is done, the boy doesn't give the girl an engagement ring but a necklace we call *lanco* in Romani. It is usually made of gold and passed down from mother to daughter to granddaughter. If they must, they can buy one. When the woman is married, she must always have something in her hair, either a *diklo* [scarf] or some kind of ribbon. This indicates to the other Rom on the street that she is married. She must also wear a long skirt, though single women can wear more modern dresses.

Men can wear anything though we don't wear tight jeans and sneakers often. And my wife never wears tight jeans. However, some of our traditions are gradually disappearing. I am a modern man but some things seemed better twenty years ago.

To get to know the Rom one has to really understand our mentality. With most *gaje* we tell them as little about us as possible. With the *gaje* we are *ditardomok*, which means "slippery." However, when I speak with you, it is as if I have known you for many years. I am open and honest with you as you are with me. With a Swede or even another American this would never happen, speaking straight from the heart and not from behind you. We like to speak with the *gaje* but we are careful. It has happened in the past that journalists have come to our homes, spoken with us, and then wrote some stuff in the newspaper about us that wasn't true. We must protect our families and our traditions.

Unfortunately there are many in Sweden who still think we should leave. This is why we live separately from them. There are racists here. When my wife and I go out sometimes, we hear Swedish people speaking about us, about our car—"Look at those Gypsies." For my grandparents, mother, father, brothers, sisters, and my children this reality is for their whole life. The *gaje* can see who we are and speak badly about us. Why? Because we don't have our own country? Because of our language? Because of the clothes we wear? We live and work for our children and our families. We have nothing else. I'll leave all my money for my children and they will do the same for their children. We can never completely extinguish this flame of fear we always carry with us. Our fear of having to suddenly leave our homes for some unknown destination.

Rinkeby, Sweden: Rom children relaxing in their courtyard in Rinkeby, a suburb of Stockholm

Budapest, Hungary: Traditional Rom instruments, the violin and cymbalom

Romale Shavale
(Gypsy Men, Gypsy Brothers)

Rom Anthem

Intro: Adagio rubato

Transcribed by Karen Elaine

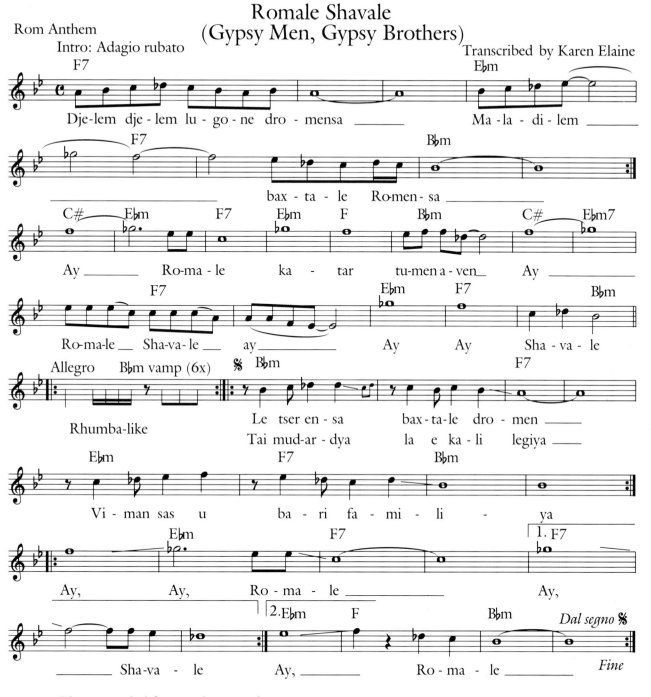

I have traveled far over long roads,
I have met lucky Gypsies.
Oh, Gypsies, from wherever you come,
With your families along fortunate byways,
I too once had a large family,
But the black legion murdered them.
Oh, Gypsy men, oh, Gypsy boys . . .

The Gypsy Anthem,
adopted 1969.
Translated by Ronald Lee,
Canadian delegate to the NGO of the UN
World Romani Union

GLOSSARY

Antwerp: The second-largest city in Belgium, after Brussels

Auschwitz: A city located near Krakow, where the largest World War II concentration/death camp was established by the Germans in 1940

Belarus: An independent country formerly known as Byelorussia, a republic of the former Soviet Union

bişaria: A necklace made of gold and silver coins that is worn in the hair of Rom women

Bratislava: The capital of Slovakia

Bukovina: Formerly a region in northern Romania. Today it is in Ukraine.

Carpathian Mountains: A mountain chain in Central Europe that extends over Slovakia, Hungary, and Ukraine and down into Romania

chara: A Romanian word meaning "crow." Used by the gaje as slang for Rom or for a dark-skinned person who steals

cholent: A traditional Eastern European Jewish Sabbath dish prepared a day ahead from potatoes, groats, beans, and meat

Cigan: The word for the Rom in Hungarian

Cortorari: Nomadic Rom tribe in Romania

cymbalom (tsimbal, zimbal, cymbal): A trapezoidal, hammered instrument. It is the great-grandfather of the piano.

diklo: A scarf worn by a Rom woman, covering her head indicating that she is married

ditardomok: Romani slang term meaning "slippery"

Gábori: A Rom tribe in Romania

gaje: Plural for non-Gypsies

gajo: Singular for non-Gypsy

galbi: Nickname for salbădegalben

Gothenburg (Göteborg in Swedish): The second-largest city in Sweden

Hodász: A town located near Nyirbátor in northeastern Hungary

Kiruna: A mining city located in the far-north province of Norrlands, Sweden.

knishes: A Jewish dish consisting of either potatoes or meat seasoned with onions, salt, and pepper stuffed into individual balls of dough

kumpania: A company of Rom that travels together

Kurds: The indigenous people of Kurdistan, a region falling within Turkey, Iran, Iraq, Syria, Armenia, Azerbaijan, and Georgia

lanco: A necklace worn by a Rom woman indicating she is engaged to be married

Lăutari: Rom tribe in Romania

lecso: A Hungarian dish consisting of eggs, tomatoes, red peppers, and paprika

Lund: A university city located near Malmö in southwestern Sweden

Makó: A city in southern Hungary near Romania

Malmö: The third-largest city in Sweden

Maramureş: A northwestern region in Romania where Satu-Mare and Sighetu Marmeţiei are located. Maramures borders the Carpathian-Ruthenian region of Ukraine.

Mátészalka: A city in northeastern Hungary

mokan: A Romani slang word used by the Romanian Rom to insult the gaje. It means "mountain person."

Moscow: The capital of Russia

Nyíregyháza: A city in northeastern Hungary

Olach: A Rom tribe in Hungary

Oradea: A city in western Transylvania, Romania

Oşer: A suburb of Cluj, Romania

palinka: Hungarian liqueur

parameetchi: Romani for long, narrative stories

phuri bibi: Rom for "old aunt"

Rom: Refers to the Gypsy people. The term is also used for a Rom man or husband.

Romani: The Rom language

Romano Paso: Rom adults

Romsal: Romani for "Are you Rom?"—a Romani greeting

Romungro: A Rom tribe in Hungary, originating from Transylvania, Romania

Ruthenians (Rusyns): An agrarian people related to the Ukrainians and who live today in Slovakia and the sub-Carpathian Ruthenia region of Ukraine

salbădegalben: A bişaria made only from gold coins

sarmi: A Rom dish consisting of hamburger, rice, and paprika stuffed into cabbage leaves

Szeged: A city located in southern Hungary near Romania

Szombathely: A city in western Hungary near Austria

Teater Romen: The Rom theater of Moscow, established in 1925

Tîrgu-Jiu: A Romanian city in the Transylvanian Alps in the province of Wallachia

Tisza River: Begins in Ukraine, flows through Hungary, and finally joins the Danube River in Serbia

Transnistria: An area between the Dniester and Bug rivers, which served as a reservation for deported Jews and Rom from Romania. Today this area is in southern Ukraine.

Transylvania: A region in western Romania

Ungvár: The Hungarian name for the Ukrainian city of Uzhgorod

Uppsala: A university city in Sweden, just north of Stockholm

vajda: Romani word meaning "the one person tribunal," or a man of authority among the Rom in Hungary

Västerås: A Swedish city west of Stockholm

vurdon: Romani for "covered wagon"

Wallachia: A province in southern central Romania

Zlátari: A Rom tribe in Romania

BIBLIOGRAPHY

BOOKS

Arnstberg, Karl Ulov, and Billy Ehn. *Etniska Minoriteter i Sverige Förr och Nu*. Lund: Liber Laromedel, 1976.

Burrow, George. *The Gypsies of Spain*. London: John Murray, 1923.

Clébert, Jean-Paul. *The Gypsies*. Translated by Charles Duff. London: Vista Books, 1963.

Djuric, Rajko, and Nebojša Bato Tomašević. *Gypsies of the World: A Journey into the Hidden World of Gypsy Life and Culture*. New York: Henry Holt, 1988.

Eriksson, Ann, and Karine Mannerfelt. *Zigenarliv: Bilder fran en Stockholms Föröt* (Gypsy Life: Pictures from a Stockhom Suburb). Sollentuna: Vudya Kitaban Förlag, 1991.

Ficowski, Jerzy. *Cyganie w Polsce: Dzceje I Obyczaje* (Gypsies in Poland: People and Culture). Warsaw: Wydawnictwo Interpress, 1989.

Lo-Johansson, Ivar. *Zigenare* (Gypsies). Stockholm: Bokförlaget Prisma, 1963.

Svensk Uppslagsbok (Swedish encyclopedia). s.v. *"Gypsy."* Malmö: Förlagshuset Norden AM, 1959.

Sway, Marlene. *Gypsy Life in America: Familiar Strangers*. Urbana, Ill. University of Illinois Press, 1988.

Tong, Diane. *Gypsy Folk Tales*. San Diego: Harcourt Brace Jovanovich, 1989.

ARTICLES

Hancock, Ian. "Uniqueness of the Victims: Gypsies, Jews and the Holocaust." *Without Prejudice: The EAFORD International Review of Racial Discrimination* 1, no. 2 (1988):45–67.

Ingram, Judith. "For Gypsies of Romania, Help at Last." *New York Times*, 7 August 1992.

———. "'Gypsies' Plight": Mobs, Torches and Land Disputes." *New York Times*, 12 June 1992.

Kinzer, Stephen. "Germany Cracks Down; Gypsies Come First." *The New York Times*, 27 September 1992.

Kurlansky, Mark. "A Voice of the Generation of '56." *International Herald Tribune*, 10 November 1992.

Lewin, Tamar. "Study Points to Increases in Tolerance of Ethnicity." *New York Times*, 8 January 1992.

Protzman, Ferdinand. "Germany Reaches Deal to Deport Thousands of Gypsies to Romania." *New York Times*, 18 September 1992.

———. "Music of Hate Raises the Volume in Germany." *New York Times*, 2 December 1992.

Simons, Marlise. "Forging a New Gypsy Spirit: Will Sanskrit Help?" *New York Times*, 27 August 1990.

Tagliabue, John. "Uneasy and Poorer at Home, East's Gypsies Wander West." *International Herald Tribune*, 28 November 1991.

Tyranauer, Gabrielle. "Gypsies and the Holocaust: A Bibliography and Introductory Essay." *Montreal Institute for Genocide Studies* 2 (1991): vii–xxviii.